# Advance Praise for *Aim High*

"*Aim High* is a testament to high ideals and hard work. Debbie James lived these principles during her time as Secretary of the Air Force. This book reminds us that it's not just about getting the job done, but also about HOW you do the job. I recommend *Aim High* for leaders at all levels!"

—CHUCK HAGEL, 24th Secretary of Defense, Former US Senator

"Lead several hundred thousand people, manage a budget over $100 billion, and secure the nuclear enterprise. That's what Secretary James did as the second woman ever to run the US Air Force, and this book feels like having a personal conversation with her. She takes you behind the scenes with rich case studies to share valuable leadership lessons for your career and your life."

—ADAM GRANT, Professor, Wharton School, University of Pennsylvania, LinkedIn Top Voices 2017, *New York Times* bestselling author of *Originals, Give and Take,* and *Option B*

"Debbie's insights are words to live by, and she has lived them herself over her remarkable life and career. Debbie is that rare leader who remains humble and grounded, despite her many successes, and she brings all her life lessons together in these memorable stories. *Aim High* is a must read for all who aspire to leadership positions."

—ADAM BRYANT, Bestselling Author: *The Corner Office: Indispensable and Unexpected Lessons from CEOs on How to Lead and Succeed, New York Times* and *Newsweek* Senior Editor and Columnist, CNBC Contributor, Managing Director, MERRYCK & Co.

"I have watched Debbie James navigate, extraordinarily, leadership challenges through twenty-five years as a professional colleague. *Aim High* reveals an incredible journey through the worlds of politics and executive positions in government and business. A remarkable tutorial for all seeking a role model of courage and success."

—GENERAL (RET) JOHN JUMPER, 17th Chief of Staff, United States Air Force

"Who would have thought that a leadership book could be a page-turner or that it could make you laugh and cry? That's exactly what Debbie James has achieved in *Aim High*. Part memoir, part how-to book, Secretary James has woven her professional and personal experience into advice and observations about careers and leadership to great effect. *Aim High* should be at the top of the reading list for any leadership class, or for those who want to know what authentic leadership looks like!"

—JARED COHON, 8th President, Carnegie Mellon University,
Professor, Carnegie Mellon College of Engineering

"Debbie's passion to make a difference, combined with her personal achievements in the public and private sectors, provide the context for relevant and practical leadership skills that all of us can use to aim high with a sense of purpose and navigate a course to success. Her message to all leaders is effective—set a direction, inspire others and deliver results. Debbie's approach to overcoming challenges and creating opportunities is one that all of us can relate to in our lives and careers."

—TONY MORACO, Chief Executive Officer, SAIC, Inc.

"I had the honor and pleasure of working with Debbie James when she served as Secretary of the Air Force. I saw the success of her three step leadership model as we tackled many extremely challenging issues. In *Aim High*, Debbie shares the elements of her approach in a comfortable, story-telling style. An excellent read for leaders just starting out or mid-career as they pave their personal and professional paths."

—ELLEN M. PAWLIKOWSKI, General, USAF (Retired)

"A must read for anyone leading a major organization as well as interested in personal growth. Through practical insights and case studies, Debbie James gives us a playbook for thriving in turbulent change. By writing with raw honesty and warmth, she gives us the courage to aim high!"

—SANYIN SIANG, LinkedIn Top Voices 2017, Forbes Contributor, Executive Director, Coach K Leadership and Ethics Center, Duke University

"This is a great book! We can all learn from the Secretary's approach to life, problem solving and execution. Personally, I consider Debbie to be one of my mentors. Much of how I approach problem solving was framed by her. I am thankful for her service, intellect, friendship and leadership."

—JOHN ROGERS, Chief Executive Officer, EO, RL Leaders,
Former CEO, MV Transportation

# AIM HIGH

# AIM HIGH

## CHART YOUR COURSE AND FIND SUCCESS

### DEBORAH LEE JAMES

Post Hill
PRESS

A POST HILL PRESS BOOK

Aim High:
Chart Your Course and Find Success
© 2019 by Deborah Lee James
All Rights Reserved

ISBN: 978-1-64293-034-4
ISBN (eBook): 978-1-64293-035-1

Interior design and composition by Greg Johnson, Textbook Perfect

**Post Hill Press**
New York • Nashville
posthillpress.com

Published in the United States of America

# CONTENTS

# FOREWORD

IMAGINE WHAT IT'S LIKE TO LEAD A BRANCH OF THE US military—to make life-and-death decisions that affect millions of people around the world. Imagine you're a civilian responsible for hundreds of thousands of people in uniform. Imagine you're a woman in charge of a fighting force that is overwhelmingly male.

Deborah Lee James knows very well what it's like. And she wants everyone to benefit from her wisdom and experience.

As Secretary of the US Air Force, her success was America's success. She dealt with urgent national security issues, from the safety of our nuclear weapons to the readiness of our National Guard to the quality of our air defense. She was entrusted with immense power and responsibility, and she served with both honor and skill.

I met Secretary James—or Debbie, as she insists on being called—thanks to Lean In. My nonprofit runs Lean In Circles, small groups of peers who gather regularly to support one another and learn together. For women in the military, Circles can be a much-needed source of encouragement and understanding. I will never forget the officer who told me that she wasn't scared at all to jump out of an airplane into enemy territory, but she was terrified to bring up gender issues with her commanding officer. Circles empower women to have those conversations—and therefore make change more likely.

As one of the top women in the US Armed Forces, Debbie was determined to make the military a better place for women and everyone. One day in 2015, she joined me for a Circle meeting at the Pentagon. I was struck by how attentively she listened to what every person in that room had to say, no matter what their rank or branch of service. A few weeks later, Debbie launched a Circle of her own. Then she launched another one. For the rest of her time as Secretary, Debbie met with her two Circles—one for officers, one for enlisted personnel—every month. It sent a powerful signal to the entire US military that this leader sought their input, was attuned to their needs, and was invested in their success.

Today, Debbie is back to being a private citizen. She's now on the advisory board of *Lean In*. And *Lean In*'s military chapter has more than two thousand members and counting, based everywhere from Minnesota to South Korea.

Leadership takes many forms. Deborah James followed her own brand of leadership all the way to the highest levels of public service and the private sector. She believes in collaboration, not bullying; openness, not secrecy; responsibility, not passing the buck. This book reflects those values. It is full of frank, relatable advice for how to overcome setbacks, steer yourself through crises, balance work and family, and serve with honor.

If you've ever wondered how to aim high and achieve your dreams, Debbie's book will show you how.

*Sheryl Sandberg*
Chief Operating Officer, Facebook
Founder of LeanIn.Org
Founder of OptionB.Org

# INTRODUCTION

B Y MID-JANUARY 2014, I WAS THREE WEEKS INTO A BRAND-NEW job—the biggest job of my life. As the twenty-third Secretary of the Air Force, I had become only the second woman in history to lead a branch of the US military. Although I was hesitant about taking on this role in the first place, my doubts had begun to subside. I had a hundred-day plan, three priorities, and a travel schedule designed to highlight the important themes and actions I wanted to pursue. Overall, not bad for less than a month on the job. Or so I thought....

Just then, it seemed like all hell broke loose.

You see, while working in my palatial office overlooking the Potomac River and the monuments of Washington, I received a classified email—bad news. There had been an irregularity in personnel testing of one of the units out west in charge of our nuclear intercontinental ballistic missiles. Some of the young officers—called missileers—who stood watch over these important and destructive weapons—were found to have cheated on a basic proficiency exam. The whole thing became known during a drug investigation when cell phones were confiscated. It was discovered that test answers had been passed by some in the unit to others.

Although the information was sketchy at this time, I knew the situation was serious.

Nuclear weapons are obviously the most catastrophically destructive weapons in the US arsenal. In light of the information I just learned, I questioned, "Is the nuclear enterprise safe and secure?" If young missileers cheated on exams, and if some were taking drugs, did this mean they were unfamiliar and unable to perform their duties should a real-world event present itself?

I wasn't immediately sure what to do about this firestorm on the horizon, but I did know that it was up to me to figure it out, and fast.

As I said, I had some hesitation about taking on the assignment of Secretary of the Air Force. To be sure, I was flattered by President Obama's offer. I had devoted my entire professional life to the national security of the United States and being Secretary of the Air Force was, in many ways, a dream come true.

And let's face it, it's hard to turn down the President of the United States.

But I knew that transitioning from my job at SAIC, a Fortune 500 government contractor where I led a $2 billion-dollar unit, to a government position would be tough and risky.

First, I had worked hard to get where I was at SAIC—one of the most senior leaders of the company (and one of the few senior women) responsible for roughly 8,700 employees who supported government customers in areas like hardware integration, software development, and logistics management.

I loved what I was doing and was not anxious to give it up! Although I did not have an MBA, I had become a successful businesswoman, achieving or exceeding my goals for growth, profitability, program excellence, customer satisfaction, and employee engagement.

Before SAIC, I also had a successful government career. In the 1990s, I served as the Assistant Secretary of Defense for Reserve Affairs, one of a handful of top policy advisors to the Secretary of Defense. So I was no stranger to the Pentagon. Talk about being one of the few senior women in a sea of male colleagues—the Pentagon was it in those days! And the fact that I was young (thirty-four years old) and had never served in uniform set me apart even more.

Despite these challenges, during the five years I served in that job, I led a major transformation on how our part-time forces—the National Guard and Reserves—were utilized within the military. They went from being considered "weekend warriors," who were called upon only during periods of all-out war, to "integral operational assets," available in day-to-day operations short of war.

I was also very familiar with the operations of the US Congress—and the relationship Congress has with the Executive branch. That's because I worked for one of the major defense committees—the House Armed Services Committee—for ten years. I started out as an intern and worked my way up to one of the most senior staff positions. I assisted the powerful committee chair with a host of issues—ranging from personnel issues to weapons procurement.

The bottom line for me, at this point in my life, was that I was comfortable in my skin and with what I had already achieved in both government and business. I felt accomplished and personally fulfilled by my work, and I saw myself remaining in the business world until my eventual retirement.

Until, that is, President Obama's offer to lead the Air Force came along.

Then I had to ask myself: Do you really want to risk a return to the Pentagon? There were some serious drawbacks to consider.

First, I would have to say hello to a big pay cut if I returned to government. My annual compensation at SAIC was way more than I ever dreamed possible in my younger years, and I had acquired stock and stock options that I knew would have to be divested or forfeited.

Second, I would have to come back up to speed on old issues and learn completely new ones. I'm talking about policy matters ranging from personnel and compensation issues affecting members of the military—a subject I was well-versed in but dated—to the intricacies of new weapons systems, like the F35 fighter aircraft—something I knew relatively little about.

Third, bureaucratic battles in the Pentagon and Capitol Hill to resolve policy and budget disputes were familiar territory to me, but did I have the drive to get back into the political fray?

And finally, what if I stumbled in some public way? Or what if there was some sort of scandal on my watch for which I was blamed?

As far as I was concerned, the latter concern was the most daunting—I had watched good people work hard and successfully their whole lives, then assume senior government posts, devote enormous time and energy, only to have something really bad happen on their watch that sent their reputation of a lifetime out the window.

(Now do you understand why the nuclear cheating scandal seemed like a really big deal?)

Although I had always operated as one of few women in a heavily male-dominated field, becoming Secretary of the Air Force was a major cut above anything I had ever done before. Would a civilian national security professional who never served in uniform, and a woman at that, be accepted by the male-dominated institution of the uniformed military? Could I perform the job to a high degree of excellence and earn the respect of those I would be leading? Could I accomplish important goals for the Air Force at a time of unprecedented divisiveness and dysfunction in Washington?

I had no idea where all of this would lead me, but after a lot of soul searching, I took the leap of faith and plunged head-first into preparing for—and then doing—the job.

In case you are not familiar with the position of Secretary of the Air Force, let me offer a little context on what the job entails.

Being "SECAF" is, in many ways, like being the CEO of a major corporation. As Secretary, and like a CEO, I was responsible for people, training, technology investments, asset procurement (weapons systems), facilities, and executing on the mission. Our mission—unlike any other on earth—was to fly, fight, and win in the air, space, and cyber space in support of military operations around the world. As you read the news every day, events in Syria, Afghanistan, Iraq, Europe, the Korean peninsula, Africa, and natural disasters in the US capture the headlines. They remind us of the unsettled and tumultuous world we live in. The US Air Force is at the forefront of all these operations to protect Americans and American interests abroad and at home. Whenever airpower is needed—and it always is—the President of the United States calls 1-800 US AIRFORCE. And my job—from late 2013 to early 2017— was to ensure that we were ready and able to respond. For unlike any CEO, my decisions could have meant life or death for real people.

This job gave new meaning to high stakes.

And when I say the Air Force is like a major corporation, I mean a huge corporation. We had roughly 660,000 people supporting our missions, including full-time active duty, part-time National Guard and reserve, and civilian personnel. Our assets included roughly six thousand aircraft and more than seven hundred basing locations in more than seventy different countries and territories. The Air Force is also responsible for the majority of satellites in orbit, much of the cyber protection mission for the military, and two thirds of US nuclear forces, namely the land-based intercontinental ballistic missiles (ICBM) and the bomber force.

Our $139 billion-dollar budget was larger than the GDPs of 127 countries, plus every state and territory in the United States. And our Board of Directors was the large and unwieldy group (535 members to be exact) called the US Congress, which had the power to fund, defund, direct, stop, or modify any program or action we might take.

Washington, D.C. was, and is, an ever-changing, divisive, and dysfunctional place to work. The Congress, in particular, is extremely polarized and each member is always looking to the next election cycle when it comes to casting votes about important national policies. Most disappointing of all, Congress and the White House have lost the ability to compromise, which is why our government is constantly lurching toward government shutdowns and unable to complete important work on time.

But then again, I am no stranger to dysfunction and change.

I grew up in a dysfunctional household with a single mother who was emotionally abusive to her children and who repeatedly placed us in the middle of disputes she had with our father.

I am a veteran of corporate America, which has and will continue to undergo constant change: change to innovate, change to reduce costs, and change to disrupt competitors.

And although I have had many wonderful managers and working environments, I have had two bad bosses and difficult relationships to work through.

The truth is that dysfunction and change abound in America in many ways, from the continuous turbulent change in the business environment, to our government that has become paralyzed and unable to fulfill some of the most basic requirements, to the deep and dark personal dysfunctions within ourselves, our colleagues, families, and friends.

How can someone survive—let alone thrive—in such an environment?

Though I don't have all the answers, I do have a formula that has worked for me. Not everyone deals with the nuclear enterprise, but you and I have more in common than you think. We have difficult challenges in the workplaces, inner fears about our own capabilities, relationships gone wrong, disappointments, joy, and accomplishments.

(Incidentally, I won't leave you hanging forever on the nuclear story. Keep reading—there's a lot more to this one!)

*Aim High* is the Air Force motto—it's also a deeply personal mantra for me because it captures in two short words how I've tried to lead my life through periods of ups and downs.

And because I have always learned so much about what works and doesn't work in the real world of business and government by listening to the stories of others, *Aim High* is largely a book of stories—my stories—each of which makes a point and provides insight about the essential actions and strategies for success.

In addition to the stories, you will see "data boxes" at the end of most chapters, which amplify my points through examples from the world of business.

These data boxes reinforce the fact that, although my stories are unique to me, we share more than meets the eye. I hope that readers will find the insights contained within the data boxes especially insightful—I know I did.

Today, I serve on corporate boards and non-profit boards. I also serve as a Special Advisor to Bain & Company, a top tier management-consulting firm that supports business leaders on strategy, marketing, organization, digital transformation, M&A, and operations. I am most grateful to Bain for developing the "data boxes" through their research as well as the research of others. Bain members Jen Hayes, Melissa Artabane, and Shalini Chudasama deserve tremendous credit, not only for their input to *Aim High*, but also for leading Bain's Global Women's Leadership Council— an organization dedicated to helping women thrive (personally and professionally) and to keeping Bain at the forefront of gender diversity research and workplace initiatives.

Finally, I wish to dedicate *Aim High* to the men and women of the United States Air Force. I am forever grateful for their sacrifice and accomplishments. And I am immensely proud to have worked by their side as part of the greatest Air Force on the planet.

# AIM HIGH

# CHAPTER 1

# The BLUF

A TYPICAL DAY FOR ME AT THE PENTAGON WOULD START EARLY at the gym—usually around 6:30 a.m. By eight, I would wind my way through the halls of the Pentagon to the fourth-floor corridor where my office—and those of other senior Air Force officials— were located. Because two sets of glass doors bookend this section, airmen refer to this area as "within the glass doors." You might call it the "head shed" of the Air Force.

I distinctly remember arriving within the glass doors on my first day and seeing the portraits of the twenty-two Secretaries of the Air Force who had preceded me. These paintings were both elegant and a little spooky at the same time. Their eyes seemed to follow me as I walked along, and I was filled with a sense of history. I had lots of big shoes to fill. And all of those shoes, but for one pair, belonged to men.

By eight-thirty or nine, my first meeting would start. Indeed, life at the Pentagon was filled with back-to-back meetings, and it seemed like all meetings—no matter the subject—had one thing in common: the PowerPoint brief. Whether the matter was decisional or for information only, whether it dealt with personnel policy or a weapons program review, PowerPoint covered it all.

Some days felt like death by PowerPoint.

The only thing that made this tolerable for me was the BLUF, an acronym that means Bottom Line Up Front. You see, every PowerPoint briefing began with one slide that summarized the main takeaways of the presentation before diving into many additional slides with background, reams of data, and proof points.

Stated another way, the BLUF offered an important summary early on, which always helped me tremendously, as I worked through the supporting material of the briefing.

That's why I want to begin *Aim High* with a story that summarizes the BLUF.

This story also happens to answer a question I am asked a lot: How is someone chosen to be Secretary of the Air Force? And how can any one person possibly lead and inspire 660,000 people and manage a $139 billion-dollar budget?

Here's how it went down for me.

By early February 2013, I had been with the government contractor SAIC for more than a decade. I was one of two Group Presidents, responsible for managing two billion dollars in revenue—about half of the company's business. And it was an exciting time at the company. Our Board of Directors had decided that we would "spin" SAIC into two separate, public companies, and I was playing a major role in the architecture of the new SAIC.

I was sitting behind my desk on a Friday afternoon reviewing an important presentation related to the spin when the telephone rang and interrupted my train of thought.

Collin McMahon, an Obama Personnel official at the White House, was calling.

I knew Collin through a mutual friend who served with me back in the 1990s as part of the Clinton Administration. Collin called me from time to time over the years to "brainpick" about personnel searches he was conducting.

Collin's conversations usually went something like this: "Hi Debbie—I am searching for a candidate (who has the following qualities) to serve in a senior position within government. Do you know anyone to recommend?"

Or like this: "Hi Debbie. We are vetting "Joe Smith" for a position of trust within the Administration. Do you know "Joe" and what do you think of him?"

But on this particular Friday, the conversation went like this: "Hi Debbie. I am under the gun to get a list of candidates to President Obama by Monday evening for consideration to be the next Secretary of the Air Force. I think YOU would be great in this role. Do I have your permission to include your name on the slate of candidates I send to the President?"

I just about slid off of my chair. This truly was a bolt out of the blue, but I was enormously flattered and honored. So, of course, I said yes.

"Great," he said. "I'll get back to you within the next week or two on next steps, assuming President Obama approves the list."

No sooner did I hang up the phone than doubts began to enter my mind. In the first place, who calls someone on a Friday afternoon when the list is due Monday?

Talk about putting something off until the last minute.

I quickly googled to see who was being speculated about for the position. Indeed, there were fine candidates mentioned in the press. I figured Collin called me at the eleventh hour because he needed one more name to complete his list.

This thing had to be pre-baked, and I didn't stand a chance. *But so what?* I reasoned. It's still a huge honor to have your name included on a list of candidates to be considered by the President for such an important position. I went home that night and told Frank (my then fiancée) but told no one else, because I was so sure the whole thing was going nowhere.

Over the next few weeks, Senator Chuck Hagel went through a bruising confirmation process to become the Secretary of Defense. After he was finally confirmed by the Senate and assumed the office, things started happening on my end. Collin called again and told me that the President had approved the list of contenders and that I should be ready to receive a call from the Pentagon about interviews.

And so it began.

In my first interview, I was expecting to meet the Deputy Secretary of Defense, Ash Carter, who I knew from the Clinton Administration. When I arrived, however, I was told that the Deputy had been called away suddenly and, instead, I would meet with two special assistants.

(I said to myself, "I knew this thing was rigged all along!")

The special assistants and I had a good conversation, and they asked my views on everything from relations with Congress, to the defense budget, to sexual assault in the military, to weapons systems that had run over time and over budget. I stressed that my approach to the job—just like any other job—would be to chart a course based on the key objectives of the department, play to my strengths, assemble a solid team and, above all else, get things done.

Stated another way, I knew that people issues, training and modernization concerns, and gaining efficiencies within the Department of Defense were hot topics for the Administration and with the Congress—so I would chart a course to make a difference in each of these areas.

In addition, because I knew a lot about the defense budget, the Congressional process, how to maneuver within the halls of the Pentagon, and the business end of defense, I considered these attributes to be my strengths. So I would play to these. On the other hand, because I had never served in uniform, let alone in combat, I would never try to "outdo" a combat pilot on matters of combat. This is just one example, but it goes to the point that no one knows everything—that's why the team is so important.

Finally, getting things done is what everyone is or should be about—I offered some specific examples of my problem solving approach from previous assignments.

Much to my disbelief, I was called back about a week later, finally, to see the Deputy Secretary, but once again, he was called away suddenly at the last minute. So I met more special assistants. I went home after this second appointment convinced that I had reached the end of the line.

But then I received a third call back. This time I was to see the new Secretary of Defense, Chuck Hagel. The appointment was set for 6:00 p.m. on a Friday evening. At this point, I knew things were getting serious. I didn't know how many candidates the Secretary would be interviewing, but I was pretty sure it was two or three, not four or five.

I arrived at the Pentagon at 5:45 p.m. on the appointed Friday and was shown to a waiting room. It's always a bad idea for me to drink coffee at that hour of the day, but I was nervous, so I accepted cup after cup. The hour was getting later and later. Finally, I was ushered into the Secretary's office at 7:30 p.m.

Secretary Hagel was extremely apologetic. He said he regretted ruining my night and possibly my weekend. He went on to explain that it had been "a hell of a day around here" because North Korean leader Kim Jong-Un had made some menacing moves, and Secretary Hagel made the decision just hours earlier to move more missile defense systems to the West Coast of the United States.

I said, "It's quite alright, Mr. Secretary. Nothing I had going on even begins to approach the day you have had!"

After a forty-five-minute conversation, I departed—only to be called again by one of the special assistants on Monday morning. Secretary Hagel wanted references!

And then on Friday, Collin from White House personnel called again. He was pretty cagey at first—asked me how I was doing and what was going on. I began to recount the story of the various appointments at the Pentagon culminating with my Secretary Hagel meeting.

"But wait," I said. "Don't you know any of this?"

"Yes," he replied. "I know all of it. I'm not sure exactly what you told these people, but it must have been good, because I'm calling today to ask you to quit your job. The President of the United States wants you to be the twenty-third Secretary of the Air Force!"

Years later, after we both left government, I asked Secretary Hagel why he had selected me for this important role. He told me that he was impressed with my previous work experience, my belief in teamwork, and my action orientation. He didn't use the precise expression, but I thought to myself: that's the BLUF!

I'VE LEARNED THROUGHOUT MY LIFE that there are three essential actions for achieving professional success and personal fulfillment. All take time, and there are strategies within each that should be followed.

This approach worked for me, and it will work for you too. Here's the BLUF:

1. Chart and Navigate Your Path

2. Inspire and Lead Teams

3. Get Things Done

In the pages that follow, I will tell you my story....

▸ How I **Charted and Navigated My Path**, zig-zagged with the changing environment, found joy and purpose from my work, reinvented myself along the way, and through ups and downs, achieved a wonderful family life.

▸ I'll also tell you again and again that the secret weapon for almost every challenge relates to getting the people part of the equation right and leading within a team framework. That's why learning to **Inspire and Lead Teams** is so essential, why communication is crucial, and why you should never compromise on ethics.

▸ Finally, **Get Things Done** is what we all strive to do. Whether your goals relate to a personal, business, or government challenge, there are universal steps to problem solving that everyone can follow. I'll tell you about my five-step approach and how it worked through real case studies—challenges I tackled when I was Secretary of the Air Force. I'll not only explain how the nuclear challenge played out, but also describe efforts to combat sexual assault in the military, make the Air Force more diverse (including the timely debate about transgender individuals in the military), and rid the organization of unnecessary red tape, training, and paperwork.

Taken together, the three essentials of *Aim High: Chart Your Course and Find Success* lay out practical advice you can use to navigate your challenges and ultimately achieve your life's goals.

OK, let's get to it!

How does all of this work in the real world?

# CHART AND NAVIGATE YOUR COURSE

# CHAPTER 2

# Make a Plan A,
# But Prepare to Zig-Zag

IT'S ESSENTIAL TO MAP OUT WHERE YOU WANT TO GO IN LIFE. IF you have no roadmap, you will simply drift. A big part of *Aim High* is having aspirations, so look around you for people or professions you admire and then create a plan.

But you must also realize—no matter how hard you work or how much you prepare—life will throw you curve balls. You will encounter setbacks, failures, and plain unfairness. People who you thought you could trust will sometimes let you down. When a failure, disappointment, or loss occurs, it's okay to grieve. But it's essential that you learn from each experience and bounce back as quickly as possible. Resilience is the name of the game. Have that Plan A but be prepared to pivot to Plan B quickly. This is what I call the Zig-Zag.

On the professional side, I experienced a huge zig-zag early on. Speaking plainly, my original career dream went up in smoke.

You see, throughout high school, college, and graduate school, I had one singular dream. It was my Plan A, and I charted my course methodically. I wanted to be a diplomat. So I prepared for the Foreign Service in every way I knew how: I studied Spanish in high school and was a foreign exchange student in Argentina during one summer. As an undergrad at Duke University and later in graduate school at Columbia University, I majored in International Affairs (the major at Duke was actually called Comparative Area Studies—this was the closest equivalent Duke had in those days to International Affairs). I earned top grades and perfected my Spanish skills through a college summer abroad program in Spain. I even landed a prestigious internship in the US Embassy in Lima, Peru during my first summer of grad school. (I wanted it badly, shot for the moon, and I got it!) Like I said, the Foreign Service was my Plan A.

When I left graduate school and moved to Washington, D.C., I applied to the State Department, which has both a written and oral exam. Somehow, though I thought I had everything in my favor, I was not selected.

I became so supremely disappointed that I literally crashed. I remember lying in bed for five days crying. I saw my entire young life flash in front of my eyes, and I thought I was washed up. At the ripe old age of twenty-three.

On the sixth day, I started applying elsewhere in the government (I really did want to do government work of some kind), and I desperately needed a job. Luckily, the Department of the Army hired me. While it was not exactly my heart's desire, at least it was a steady paycheck.

Although it felt bad at the time, going to the Army turned out to be the best thing that ever happened to me. You might call this my Plan B. Looking back on my life's work, I cannot imagine having had a more fulfilling career than the one I have known even if the State Department had accepted me many years ago. Today, I reflect with enormous gratitude on the zig-zags of my life!

Years later, when I was the Secretary of the Air Force, I met then-Secretary of State John Kerry. It was all I could do in this rather formal meet-and-greet session NOT to blurt out, "Thank you so much for rejecting me from the State Department decades ago."

Instead, I took the diplomatic road and chatted about the weather!

Changing professional course is not all that uncommon, particularly early on for a young adult. Some continue to pursue the original dream; indeed, sometimes these things work out okay in the end—others discover that the original Plan A was good, but that a new Plan B can be even better. I'm very fond of the expression: one door closes and another door opens. But you must have the fortitude to walk through that door. And not everyone does.

Personal zig-zags are pretty common too.

In my case, I was married twice before I finally found lasting happiness with my third husband, Frank.

I had grown up in a divorced household and the experience affected me deeply. Therefore, I was the last person who ever expected to be divorced.

But it happened.

In the first instance, the father of my children broke faith with me in an irreparable way. I went through much soul searching at the time, including counseling with family, friends, and my pastor, and concluded that it would be extremely unhealthy for my children and me to live with this deep loss of trust. So my first marriage ended after twelve years.

In the second instance, a nine-year marriage ended when my second husband left. He moved from our home in Maryland to

Florida—a dream we had discussed doing together—but he did it suddenly by himself when I needed another six months to figure out the next steps in my career. I suggested that he return so that we could try counseling or somehow work through our problems. He refused to, so, we too, divorced after a one-year separation.

To say that two unsuccessful marriages shook me to my core would be an understatement. I certainly placed a lot of blame on their shoulders. But I also began questioning everything about myself. Why had I chosen a life partner—twice—and done so poorly? What was wrong with me?

I read all the self-help books following my second divorce. After years of beating myself up, I finally decided I had not done anything fundamentally wrong. Sometimes people change, sometimes they let you down, sometimes you don't see the other person's true colors until you are already married, and sometimes there is insufficient "stick-to-it-iveness" required to have a long-term relationship. And sometimes that's for the best. It was for me. After all, my life would have been very different if I had retired to Florida in 2007!

I also realized that I could have done some things better or differently, and I've tried to live these "lessons learned" every day of my new life with Frank:

For example, I learned to:

▶ Express appreciation liberally—even for small things.

▶ Agree to disagree, without holding a grudge, and to let go of certain hot-button topics unless they are crucial.

▶ Accept my partner as he is (and he must do the same for me). The habits of a lifetime are unlikely to change fundamentally—just because you want them to.

And so I came to understand through the years that an important part of charting your course is to prepare—or at least be open to—an alternate course.

When things go wrong in your professional or personal life—as inevitably they will—take some time to reflect and grieve, but try not to take too long and try not to beat yourself up too much. The resilience to bounce back, pivot from Plan A to Plan B, and learn as many positive lessons from a negative experience—all of these skills are essential for navigating the zigs and zags of life.

## ASPIRATION/CONFIDENCE AND RESILIENCE

One key to successful zigging and zagging is aspiration and confidence. Unfortunately, research from Bain & Company suggests that women's aspiration and confidence to reach senior leadership roles start out strong but then lag their male peers mid-career, just at the point when they are making key career moves. This confidence gap has many implications: women, for example, are 41 percent more likely to believe they do not have the same opportunities for advancement as men and are 16 percent more likely to have at least one time in which they questioned their ability to be successful.

Bain found that those who do have aspiration and confidence—and therefore are more likely to withstand the zigging & zagging often required to get to a top role—share several common experiences:

▸ They believe they will make it. They believe that they have the skills and leadership to advance, and that they are more capable than their peers to take on the next role.

▶ They are inspired when they look at those before them. They are energized by leaders of their organization, and see senior managers of the firm as people to emulate.

Another key to the successful zig-zag is resilience—the ability to recover from adversity. As Sheryl Sandberg and Adam Grant write in *Option B, Facing Adversity, Building Resilience and Finding Joy*, resilience is a skillset that can be developed over a lifetime, and there are concrete steps we can take to build resilience each day.
These include:

▶ Express gratitude for the good things you have in life.

▶ Take steps to remind yourself that deep grief and pain are not permanent.

▶ Practice self-compassion to build personal confidence.

# CHAPTER 3

# Be Part of Something Big

To me, the most fulfilling purpose in life is when you can contribute to the betterment and well-being of others. Ultimately, this means being part of an endeavor that is bigger than you are. I know this sounds very cliché, but I believe it's true. If you're just working for the paycheck or to advance your own singular interests, you are less likely to feel satisfied and fulfilled with your life. Purpose is a big part of charting your course.

Purpose comes in infinite shapes and sizes and is completely dependent on individual preferences. My original idea about my own purpose was to serve the people of the United States through work in foreign policy—international trade, the movement of people, spread of democracy, that sort of thing. But as I told you, it didn't work out for me.

By the way, I think most people don't start out as young people either knowing what their purpose is or being able to achieve it. That's OK. That's also why the Zig-Zag is so important. There are many industries and careers that can serve others and inspire you if you open your eyes and are willing to learn about them. The key is: your life's work (be it working outside the home, being an at-home, full-time parent, or volunteering in some capacity) needs to jazz YOU—and the most likely way to make that happen is to find something that contributes to the betterment and well-being of others.

To be sure, making money is also important, but it's by no means the most important element in finding your purpose. I have had a variety of jobs, some more lucrative than others, and I can honestly say that the most fulfilling work was that which was not the highest paid.

Since that first debacle with the State Department, my life's purpose has been to work on military issues within the national security space—first with the Department of the Army, followed by working on the staff of the Armed Services Committee of the US House of Representatives, to being an Assistant Secretary of Defense, to years in the private sector working for firms supporting the military, to serving as the Secretary of the Air Force, to what I do now: serving on Boards of Directors, consulting through Bain & Company and working with non-profits, like LeanIn.org. All this amounts to about twenty years of government and seventeen years of private sector work.

Speaking of purpose in my private sector career, one of my proudest periods happened under some unusual circumstances.

2007 was a year from hell for me. This was the year my second husband left, my older brother, Gene, died of cancer, and the unit I led at SAIC was reorganized. The company reorganization triggered me to move from the Washington, D.C. area to Charleston, South Carolina, a beautiful city that many people would jump at the chance to live in.

I didn't feel much like jumping, though. Rather, I felt profound sadness and grief from the death of my brother, the dissolution of my marriage, and now a major job change. I nearly packed it in and left SAIC altogether, but, in the end, I decided to take a chance and forced myself to walk through this new open door.

I bought a new house in Mount Pleasant, South Carolina, rented the house in Chevy Chase, Maryland where I had lived for twenty-six years, and moved a few weeks before Thanksgiving. I rushed to unpack all my boxes before my children, Sam and Regina, then in college, and Regina Gail, my sister, arrived.

Everyone arrived for the holiday and loved the new house! My spirits were up, and I drove all of us around Charleston on a sightseeing excursion.

Literally, with my children and sister in the car, I took an important phone call.

SPAWAR (a division of the Navy and SAIC's principal customer in Charleston) had just been tapped by the Department of Defense (DOD) to take on the number-one program in DOD designed to save American lives on the battlefields of Iraq—something called the Mine Resistant Ambush Protected program—MRAP for short. Because most of our troops were dying due to the blast effects of roadside bombs (called improvised explosive devices [IEDs] by the military), then Secretary of Defense Bob Gates ordered that a new blast resistant vehicle program be initiated rapidly so that our troops could operate more safely in the future. One (and eventually multiple) vehicle manufacturers were tapped to produce the blast resistant vehicles, while SPAWAR was tapped to install all the command and control equipment, perform testing and push the vehicles to either the Charleston Air Force Base or seaport for shipping to the Middle East.

And you guessed it—the contractor workforce that performed the bulk of the work under SPAWAR was my new business unit at SAIC.

This turned out to be the most exciting, important, and high-stakes program I had ever worked on, at least up until that point in my life. I really felt a high sense of purpose on this one—and so did the rest of the workforce—because our efforts directly contributed to saving the lives of our troops.

Over the course of my three and a half years in Charleston, our team worked on thirty thousand MRAP vehicles for the Army, Marine Corps, Navy, Special Operations Command, and Air Force. We were under intense pressure to produce fifty per day in a short period of time, which required us to hire hundreds of people and establish an assembly line operation in short order. Over time, we were visited by SAIC's CEO and Board of Directors, the Secretary of Defense, and all manner of Congressmen and Senators who wanted to see the operation. Whenever a VIP visited, it was customary to stop work for about fifteen minutes so that the official could address the workforce.

To be honest, after a few years, we had received so many visitors, listening to the remarks of VIPs became pretty old.

With one major exception.

Hands down, the most inspiring address came from two very junior individuals—an Army Private and a Staff Sergeant. They visited SPAWAR's facility and spoke to our workforce in a way that none of the senior notables could ever do.

And they had an unbelievable story to tell.

The sergeant began, "We were deployed to Iraq and travelling in a convoy to our destination. The hair on the back of my neck was standing on end. It was as though I had a premonition something bad was going to happen that day. Sure enough, halfway through the day, we hit the IED."

The private continued, "The vehicle was blown more than ten feet into the air. We were belted-in but pretty beat up afterward, just the same. I blacked out but when I came to, there was smoke everywhere, and my buddy was pulling me out of the vehicle. I wasn't sure who was alive and who hadn't made it at that point. Everything was a daze."

The sergeant concluded the story, "There were some bad injuries that day, but thanks to your efforts and the MRAP, all of us lived to go home to our families. We will be forever grateful for what you did for us. Thank you for saving our lives."

At that moment, I was bursting with pride. I looked around at the rest of the workforce.

There was not a dry eye in the house—including my own.

And I knew that, in the future, as I charted and navigated my next professional move, I would continue to seek or accept assignments in which the sense of purpose felt strong.

I also knew early in my life that I wanted a personal purpose—and that focus would be children.

As I said earlier, I have been in the workforce for more than three decades, but along the way, I raised two amazing human beings. There were years I did so as a married parent and other years I did so as a single parent. You'll hear more about Sam and Regina—and how a busy and ambitious professional can successfully navigate the work/life balance—in Chapter 7.

For now, suffice it to say: none of it was easy, all of it was worth it, and I wouldn't trade either my professional or personal purpose for anything.

## DOES PURPOSE HAVE A BUSINESS CASE?

Having a greater purpose and finding meaning in your work drives inspiration in an organization and its workers. While some of us have known this all along, a study by WorkplaceTrends.com suggests that the up-and-coming workforce of millennials are perhaps even clearer about needing purpose. Millennials are gravitating towards transformational leaders who use purpose and excitement to challenge and inspire them.

Having inspired workers in an organization drives many benefits, based on research by Bain & Company:

- ▶ Inspired workers are more than twice as productive as employees who are only satisfied and three times more productive than workers who are dissatisfied.

- ▶ Focusing on inspiration drives greater commitment, satisfaction, and productivity in an organization and lowers attrition.

Unfortunately, women are 20 percent more likely to feel uninspired by their day-to-day work as men. Lack of leaders to emulate and not feeling confident enough to reach senior leadership are significant factors that result in women not advancing as far in their careers.

# CHAPTER 4

# Get A Mentor, Be A Mentor, Build Your Network

THERE IS NO DOUBT IN MY MIND THAT I AM WHAT I AM TODAY thanks in large part to the support of mentors and my network. This group is largely a collection of people I met through different work environments but also includes some school friends and neighbors. I learned how to follow, work within a team environment, inspire, and ultimately, lead others, in part, by listening and watching them.

My network is diverse in nature, that is, not everyone looks like me or comes from the same background as me. I have found new job opportunities and received good advice from my network. Many are now personal friends and have reached out to me during times of personal crisis.

A mentor can be anyone who is doing something you aspire to do—someone from whom you can learn and who can expose you to people and experiences you might not otherwise see. Finding a mentor can be as easy as asking someone to share a cup of coffee with you. (That worked for me!) And it's really important that you pay mentorship forward as soon as you reach a point in your career when you can help someone else.

Lucky for me, I met some of my most important mentors early in life, beginning with my first job in the Department of the Army, and I remain close with some of them to this day.

Back in the early 1980s, around the time of the State Department rejection, I was a liberal-minded New Jersey girl who never had any exposure to the military. (My Dad was a World War II vet, but like many of his generation, he shied away from discussing his experiences during the war.)

Consequently, I never thought about or considered a career with the military—until, of course, I was thrust in that direction.

But now, as a brand-new GS-9 Program Analyst with the Department of the Army in September, 1981, I was determined to give it my all.

So I embraced my new work—and guess what?—in relatively short order, remarkable things started happening for me.

First of all, the work turned out to be extremely interesting. Even though I was the most junior member of the team, I could see a little bit of my work contributing to the important national security issues of the day. (In the early 1980s, President Reagan was building up the military in his "peace through strength" doctrine designed to counter the threat of the Soviet Union. My Army job related to the tradeoff between resources and capabilities. In other words, for every additional dollar spent in some area, how much more capability the Army would gain in order to counter the Soviet threat).

That struck me as a really important purpose.

I also had a great boss and a great set of colleagues at the Army. This turned out to be my first experience with the power of mentorship, the importance of building and valuing a network and teamwork.

My first boss—Major General Bob Bergquist—not only took an interest in my career, he opened a door for me to do an internship on the professional staff of the House Armed Services Committee—known as the HASC. Staff members in Congress, by the way, are very powerful people. In the development of massive pieces of legislation, totaling thousands of pages each, the elected Congressmen and Senators get personally involved with a mere fraction of the issues and the language. The staff members handle the rest, using best judgment, in order to iron out the details. I was one of those.

While I was still an intern on the HASC, I attended a seminar with different speakers from different parts of the national security apparatus. One of those speakers was a man named Bob Kimmitt, an Army Major assigned to the National Security Council (NSC) staff in the Reagan White House. I thought his job sounded fascinating. He and his team were responsible for coordinating positions across the federal government on security assistance issues (for example, the sale of aircraft, weapons, and training to allies and partners around the world), as well as serving as a liaison between Congress and the NSC. I decided to approach him.

I stood in line to meet him as he concluded his remarks. When my turn came, I introduced myself and explained that I was able to do rotational assignments in an intern capacity.

"Would you be willing to have a cup of coffee with me so that I could learn more about your role at the NSC?" I asked.

The answer was yes.

That cup of coffee not only turned into a six-month stint in the Reagan White House. It also produced a lifelong mentorship and friendship with Bob Kimmitt—a future Ambassador to Germany and Deputy Secretary of the Treasury.

I then received an offer to join the staff of the HASC full time. By then, I was twenty-five years old—my peers were all ten to twenty years older than me and most had uniformed military experience. I would never have had a chance at landing this job had it not been for the door-opening of my first boss, General Bergquist. Like I said, the Committee got to try me out as an intern (I was still paid by the Army during this period) and then hired me into a full-time job as soon as one became available. (This turned into a ten-year role for me.)

My first boss on the HASC, Kim Wincup, a former Air Force lawyer and senior professional staff member on the Military Personnel and Compensation Subcommittee, was also a great mentor to me. He gave me extra duties, stretched me, introduced me to members of Congress and allowed me to do some Congressional travel in those early years. Kim remains a good friend and a key member of my network to this day.

That's what mentors do: they take an interest, they counsel, they open doors to opportunities and people that you might not otherwise have the chance to meet. What happens next is up to you, but the door-opening can be crucial—it certainly was for me.

To put it succinctly, mentors can help you chart your course.

And your network can help you navigate it.

My network consists of people I have "collected" in each of my job assignments: parents from my children's schools, my own schooling, my social media network (LinkedIn, and so on), and a wonderful group of women I now meet with regularly who either are serving or aspire to serve on Boards of Directors (we call ourselves B2B, which stands for Broads to Boards). Not only do many of these people represent decades-long friendships, they also have helped me as I have changed jobs and encountered challenges. Submitting a resume cold to a website can be a frustrating endeavor, frequently with no response. In my case, not since my earliest days with the Army have I ever submitted a resume cold—thanks to my network.

Finally, as soon as you are at a point in your own career in which you are able, you need to pay it forward and become a mentor yourself.

I did this at SAIC, where I started a mentoring program for high-potential employees within my business unit. My thought was: *If you are to be a senior leader in my unit, you need to share responsibility for developing the next generation of leaders.* I made mentoring a requirement for my direct reports (I did it too!) and rated their effectiveness in the role as part of their annual performance evaluation.

After becoming Secretary of the Air Force, I became active in Lean In, the movement launched by Facebook COO, Sheryl Sandberg. Lean In Circles are small, peer-to-peer groups that meet periodically to discuss challenges in the workplace and at home. Some circles are comprised only of women, while others have both women and men represented. LeanIn.org provides excellent online content to help guide the discussions.

I was so impressed with the approach that I launched two circles while I was Secretary and participated on a monthly basis with each of them. My circles had both women and men, and they helped me in a way I did not originally anticipate—they gave me another avenue to hear about issues and problems from airmen I would not otherwise meet.

And I heard repeatedly from my circle members that Lean In helped them through some tough challenges.

Here's just one example. After deploying to Afghanistan, I was thrilled to hear from Major Michael Nerenberg:

*Ma'am,*

*I arrived in Kabul at Camp RS, and it is everything I expected it to be and a lot worse. Luckily, I missed the Bagram suicide bomber by a day because my flight was delayed. This is my first time outside the US so it has been quite a bit of culture shock for me.... The weather forecast in Kabul just said "smoke."*

*I work with a group of civilian contractors who advise the local Afghan military. I serve as the deputy director of staff and go "outside the wire" with advisors and act as guardian Angel while they advise. There is a big movement to help increase and strengthen the women in the Afghan military. It's cool to see the effort and then look back at the Lean In Circle experience and see how it's being applied. I really appreciate the opportunity you gave me to be a member of the Lean In Circle as it is already paying dividends working in an office that personifies diversity....*

*Very respectfully, Michael*

Today there are more than forty thousand Lean In Circles across the world helping women and men work through challenges in government, business, and life. I am so proud to remain active with the movement today by serving on Sheryl's Lean In Advisory Board, and I'm grateful to know the people I met through our Air Force circles.

Also during my SECAF tenure, I discovered an existing tool for personnel tracking that we were able to leverage and launch as a mentoring approach. I called "My Vector"—as the tool was named—the "Match.com of mentoring," in that it allowed airmen anywhere in the world to make connections with others who were willing to provide mentorship. Over time, I mentored a total of five Air Force members—women, men, uniformed military, and civilian personnel.

I could go on with more stories but I think you get the point—get mentored and be a mentor as soon as you are able. If your organization has a formal program, that's great. If it does not, don't let that stop you. Remember: finding a mentor or being a mentor can be as easy as asking someone to have a cup of coffee. You have nothing to lose in doing so, and that might just be the start of a productive and long-term relationship for both of you.

## SPONSORSHIP: MENTORSHIP ON STEROIDS

While mentorship and networking are crucial for charting and navigating your course, sponsorship can be pivotal for workplace success, especially for women.

Forbes defines a sponsor as a senior leader who not only gives advice and counsel, but also speaks for, advocates for, and uses political capital for the sponsoree's advancement.

According to Harvard Business Review, women have more than enough mentors but are only half as likely as their male peers to have a sponsor. As a result, they fail to benefit from the sponsor effect:

▶ Without a sponsor behind them, 43 percent of men and 36 percent of women will ask their manager for a stretch assignment; with sponsor support, the numbers rise, respectively, to 56 percent and 44 percent.

▶ The majority of unsponsored men (67 percent) and women (70 percent) resist confronting their boss about a raise; with a sponsor in their corner, nearly half of men and 38 percent of women summon the courage to negotiate.

Research from Catalyst suggests that companies must explicitly communicate an expectation of sponsorship to their executives—companies need to create an environment in which sponsorship can thrive.

# CHAPTER 5

# Hang in There
# with Positivity

"**N**OBODY LIKES A DEBBIE DOWNER!" A teacher once said that to me and it stuck, (even before Saturday Night Live made a skit about it). Nothing happens quickly or smoothly in the government—frequently things don't happen quickly or smoothly in industry either. When everything around you seems like it's crashing, confused, or taking too long, it's important to hang in there with a positive attitude—at least for a while. This is especially important in leadership positions, for if you cannot see the opportunity amongst all the challenges, your team will not be able to see the opportunity either.

Moreover, when your work environment seems to take a turn for the worse because of what feels like too much change, reorganization, or dysfunction, work to embrace (or adapt to) the change—at least for a while. In other words, don't pass immediate judgment or jump ship right away. Instead, roll with it and make a change only after a reasonable passage of time if you decide that the new way is simply not for you. This advice also applies when dealing with difficult people.

Probably the toughest professional challenge for me was transitioning from the government sector to the private sector the first time around. The year was 1998, and by now, I had worked in the government for seventeen years. I was ready for a change. Once again, I was Charting my Course.

I was concluding a successful assignment as the Assistant Secretary of Defense for Reserve Affairs, a time when I learned a great deal about how to Lead and Inspire teams (you'll read some of these stories in Part II). I was the rank equivalent of a four-star general and thirty-nine years old—young enough to still have a full career in the private sector. So I charted my course, leveraged my network, and consulted with my mentors to improve my prospects for my first great assignment in the private sector. My optimism was at an all-time high.

It didn't quite happen as I had hoped or planned. More Zig-Zag moments were to come.

Although I had two good job offers when I left the Pentagon, I had a hard time finding my niche in the early years. Part of this was me (transitioning from government to the private sector is not easy) and part of it was the jobs I chose and the bosses who led the organizations.

My first job was Vice President of International Operations and Marketing for United Technologies Corporation, a top tier company specializing in aerospace and building products. The challenge was that my position was a new one, with somewhat vague responsibilities, and every time I would try to flesh out the responsibilities, it seemed I stepped on someone else's turf. To make matters worse, for the first time in my life, I was assigned to a boss who I simply could not please. She was capricious and quick-tempered. Direction given on Monday could easily change 180 degrees by Thursday without warning or explanation.

But I hung in there with a positive attitude and tried to adjust to her style. For example, I could see that she learned more through verbal communication than through writing. So I dialed the email and memos way back and made more in-person appointments to meet with her.

I also tried confirming her direction back to her—both verbally and through emails—to ensure that no misunderstanding about what she wanted would occur on my part.

After about nine months, I finally concluded that I could not make this work for me. So I began to look for another job and hung in there with a positive attitude until I found one.

Leaving United Technologies, I went from a twenty-five-thousand-person organization to a thirty-person organization when I joined the Business Executives for National Security, a small nonprofit that used the expertise of its business members to help solve government problems. I was the Chief Operating Officer to the CEO, a retired four-star general, whom I knew as a peer during my years in the Pentagon. How great was this?

As it turned out: not so much. Out of the frying pan and into the fire.

Note to self—knowing someone as a peer may be very different from working for that person as a subordinate. He was micromanaging, critical, and received feedback poorly. Within about six months, he moved from the Washington, D.C. area where the organization was headquartered but still continued to lead the organization from afar. The micromanaging became even more intense. There also were alleged inappropriate relationships within the work environment.

Once again, I hung in there with a positive attitude and tried to make it work—for a while.

This boss needed frequent communication to feel up to speed, so I would begin each day by calling him to lay out what I envisioned as the key activities and tasks of the day and then send multiple emails throughout the day with updates. I hoped all of this would satisfy his desire for regular information flow.

However, as it turned out, if I sent three emails, he said I should have sent four. If we spoke once per day, he wondered aloud why I had not also called him a second time to give him a wrap up at the end of the day.

Once again, over time, I came to understand this was not the right place for me.

By now, I was three years out of government and had not yet found my niche.

Then in the fall of 2001, shortly after September 11, 2001, my old boss and mentor from the Congress, Kim Wincup, invited me to lunch. Having lunch once a year had become a ritual for Kim and me, dating back nearly twenty years from the time we first met when I joined the committee staff. Kim now worked for a technical services and solutions contractor named SAIC, and he was helping one of the company's senior executives search for a new deputy.

I'm not sure Kim had this in mind when we booked the lunch, but by the time dessert was over, he seemed genuinely enthused about introducing me to SAIC and the deputy position. Three months later, I joined the company, where I ultimately spent the next twelve years of my working life.

Finally, my optimistic outlook rewarded me.

There's no doubt about it—the period between leaving the government and joining SAIC was a rough patch for me. To be sure, I was dealing with my own learning curve, but I also fell in with two bosses with whom the fit was just not right. But I hung in there with persistence and as much positivity as I could muster before eventually cutting the cord.

And each time I moved on, I remembered the words of my teacher from long ago: "No one likes a Debbie Downer." No new employer wants to hear a barrage of complaints about the last job—so move forward with optimism and dignity, and capture something positive out of every negative experience.

And there were positives at both locations (including some of the people with whom I remain in touch and who are now part of my network)!

From my time at United Technologies:

▶ I learned the fundamentals of doing business overseas—something that would help me in future roles in both industry and government.

From my time at the Business Executives for National Security:

▶ I learned the fundamentals of raising money—something that comes in very handy with my non-profit work today.

And from both, I learned:

▶ Perform a thorough due diligence on a new boss before accepting a position; and

▶ Take care with not only words but also with body language. Facial expressions and posture can negatively impact your best efforts to appear positive.

Years later, after I became Secretary of the Air Force, I had another major opportunity to put "Hang in there with Positivity" to work.

By way of background, one of my top jobs as SECAF was to present and defend the Air Force budget to the Congress. This was done formally through Congressional hearings and informally through meetings with members and their staff. Having served ten years on Capitol Hill, I thought this part of the job would be easy.

Wrong, wrong, wrong.

Though there are many good people on Capitol Hill, ultimately the goal of all Congressmen and Senators is to be reelected. Former Speaker of the House Tip O'Neill famously said, "All politics is local." Consequently, every member of Congress will view an official like me as someone who can either help or hurt his or her top goal.

As a result, it was not unusual for me to meet in private with a member who would be polite and solicitous toward me in the hopes that I would either protect or bring favor to a particular military base or issue that affected their state or district. And then in a public hearing—sometimes the very next day—that same member would rip me to pieces over a proposed budget reduction or policy matter.

What happened to civility? And why the Jekyll-and-Hyde approach?

The answer: Public hearings are televised, and some members want every opportunity to land a sound bite on the evening news about how they took a senior official to task and defended their district or state interests.

Needless to say, this approach felt galling, but I hung in there and never lost my cool. Not once—in private or public—did I call anyone out on the two-faced approach. And after dealing with this treatment, I would always continue to deal in good faith and demonstrate a positive attitude with these members, including through body language!

As I have said before, Members of Congress are very powerful people and they can make matters even more difficult if they go after you on a personal level. I tried not to take this treatment personally and recognize it for what it was.

This is another key learning—when dealing with a difficult personality, do your best to understand what is driving the difficult behavior. Frequently, I believe it relates back to some sort of insecurity or anxiety—which could be of a personal or professional nature.

Insecurity and anxiety are good segues to tell my final story on the importance of "Hanging in there with Positivity." This one is deeply personal and relates to my relationship with my mother.

My parents were divorced when I was six years old, following a turbulent and unhappy twenty-three-year marriage. I was the third of three children and much younger than the other two. (My brother, Gene, was sixteen and my sister, Regina Gail, was twelve when I was born.) The whole family (except me) lived near Baltimore, Maryland, but the family moved in the late 1950s to New Jersey when my father changed jobs. A chemical engineer by training, he spent two decades working for the State of New Jersey in the state equivalent of the Environmental Protection Agency. I grew up in a small town near the Jersey shore—Rumson, New Jersey.

Whereas my siblings remembered (and bore the emotional scars) of being exposed to every fight in my parents' final years of marriage, I don't remember any of that directly. My experience related more to the aftermath—living with my mother as a single parent and seeing my father on weekends.

First, let me tell you the good part. I was never beaten, starved, or otherwise physically abused. I know that both parents loved me in the best way they could. I grew up in a beautiful small town—a wealthy one at that, with one of the best public school systems in the state. We lived near the ocean—lots of beach fun every summer. Finally, my sister, Regina Gail, was my hero and role model in those early years, and we remain extremely close to this day. Back then, she worked for American Airlines, which made the otherwise expensive world of air travel accessible to me when I was a teenager. She was my original inspiration to be a diplomat, as I caught the travel bug early on.

Overall, to outsiders, we looked pretty normal, though divorce was not commonplace in the 1960s, at least not within my small-town environment.

Here's the not-so-good part. Mom was always an extremely high-strung and emotional person—she has taken some sort of anxiety or anti-depressant medication for as long as I can remember, she has never been happy, and she has always been extremely vocal with her children about her unhappiness. She never worked outside the home (never had the confidence to do so), so our income was 100 percent reliant upon child support and alimony. Dad always did what the law required, but not a penny more.

And it was never enough.

As I mentioned, we lived in a wealthy town (Rumson is one of the top ten wealthiest towns by household income in NJ), but we lived on a total income that would have qualified me for the free lunch program at school. Mom never applied for this, however, fearing that someone would find out and look down on us. Our house was modest—in a sea of much bigger and grander houses—and it was always a big fight about the house's upkeep. Who will pay to have the house painted? Who will pay to make repairs to the heating system? Who will pay for this or that? This became my personal nightmare, and I was always caught in the middle.

My "job" during my elementary school years was to be an extension of my mother with my father—to argue her case, and to try to get more money from him. (This was Regina Gail's job, too. My brother, Gene, went away to college and dropped out of touch with the family for several decades.)

For several years after my father left the household, I was not told what was happening. Rather, Mom told me that Dad took an apartment closer to where he worked, so he would not have to drive as far during the workweek. This also explained why I only saw him on weekends.

One weekend, Dad arrived to pick me up for the day's activities and said he first needed to talk to me. By now, I was eight years old, and I remember being somewhat annoyed, because this "talk" was delaying our fun times, like spending the afternoon in Asbury Park, running on the boardwalk, and playing in the arcades. Nonetheless, I sat down at our small kitchen table and listened to what Dad had to say.

"Deb, there is a lady outside who is very nice, and she is anxious to meet you. She will be going around with us today—maybe next weekend too. I think you will like her a lot. Her name is Mary. Also, we brought a surprise for you. There is a baby we want you to meet."

And with this brief, matter of fact introduction, I learned all in one fell swoop that my parents were divorced, my father had re-married, and I had a new half-sister. The next thing I remember is being in the back seat of the car with the baby and crying for what seemed like hours.

Now that there was a new family unit, my revised job on weekends had three parts. First, I was to report back to mom about what the new family was doing. How were they spending money, what did the house look like, and did they have more than us? The second part was to continue pleading our case to Dad about how we needed more. And the third part—most important of all—was to keep my mouth shut about my mom and her personal life. She made it very clear to me that I should give no information what-soever, and, if anything slipped, I would be in big trouble. Mom grilled me big time at the conclusion of every weekend to be sure I was fulfilling my missions.

Needless to say, I hated being put in the middle and told to serve as a spy—this is among the worst things you can do to a child in a divorce situation. Dad never did this to me in reverse, but he also never gave any ground on the money front and never intervened to help me. He was among the most secretive people I have ever known, which I assume was, in part, a defense he put up against my mother.

By the time my teen years arrived, I was increasingly taking on the role of being a mother to my mother, who was perpetually depressed, angry, and paranoid about people and things going on around her. When I went away to college, she was frantic to replace me with someone who would live with her because she feared loneliness. A boyfriend moved in for a while, until she became disenchanted with him, whereupon he moved out and she began seeing someone new. She called me often, crying and speaking of loneliness, but any time my sister and I would try to get her involved with hobbies, volunteer work, or new people, everything always fell flat. Nothing was ever quite right, and she found fault with every new idea that might have helped her. The complaints just kept coming our way.

By the time I reached my twenties, I was married with two chil-dren of my own, but Mom was still ever-present in my life—and becoming increasingly needy, demanding, and intense. Every-thing that happened in her life was a crisis requiring immediate attention. And if she did not get that immediate attention, she was also a master at laying the guilt on her two daughters. The issue of money—and never getting enough of it from my father—continued to be an issue, and I can remember getting into terrible fights with him in my teen years and twenties over how mom needed more. He was not a perfect man, but I look back on how I treated him during this period, and I feel guilty about it. Fortunately, I was able to fully reconcile with him before he died.

Today, Mom is ninety-four, and living in an assisted living facility. She has all the same negative tendencies, made worse by age, health, and partial dementia. She never has a kind, supportive, or appreciative word to say about anybody or anything. Certainly not about me.

Whatever I do (and I do a lot), it's not enough, it's not right, and it's not quick enough. At times, I have become so emotionally drained and frustrated, I have considered severing our relationship—that is how intense and gut wrenching our relationship has been. But I have always pulled back from that position. After all, she is my mother!

Point of fact: I believe that she has been angry with me throughout my entire life, and I have been angry with her as well.

Until fairly recently.

Thanks to some outside reading over the last few years, I have come to believe that my mother suffers from something called Borderline Personality Disorder (BPD). Although she was never formally diagnosed, she exhibits most of the symptoms of this disorder including paranoia, constant anger, and manipulative behaviors.

Finally, I have come to understand the source of her negative behavior.

Today, with my eyes wide open and this new learning, I have come to empathize with my mother more than ever before.

Don't get me wrong: I still get frustrated—every day with her remains extremely hard—but now, I understand better why she is the way she is. And with this empathy and understanding, I have gained renewed strength to continue hanging in there with as much positivity as I can muster.

Very importantly, I don't take her treatment of me personally anymore, and I no longer feel anger toward her.

As I said earlier, while it's important to learn positive lessons from good experiences, it's equally important to learn positive lessons from negative experiences.

For example, because of my relationship with my mother, I became determined to pursue a life very different from the life she led. Not only did I want a career and financial independence, I also wanted to be a different kind of parent than the one she was to me.

You might say my mother was my "anti" role model.

With all that said, Mom remembers things quite a bit differently. She views herself as having been the best mother ever. She regularly reminds me of this in direct and indirect ways and questions me all the time on why I don't do more for her, given all that she has done for me.

It will sound small, but one of the hardest things I do annually for my mother is to pick out Birthday and Mother's Day cards. Because the words in the vast majority of sentimental cards simply don't fit with our relationship, I tried getting humorous cards for a year or two, but Mom rejected them out of hand, so I reverted back to the sentimental to make her happy.

It takes me a long time to pick out these cards because most of the words feel disingenuous to me.

Here are a few Hallmark examples. "The best way to learn how to be a strong independent woman is by having one raise you."

Or: "Mom, every time we talk I'm filled with so many good feelings about the connection we share. I realize how lucky I am to have a mom who cares about the things going on in my life."

Or even this one: "Some years we share more laughs and other years we need more hugs. But the beautiful thing is that our relationship is always something we can depend on. I am so lucky to have you."

This year, I ended up bypassing all of these verses and instead settled on this one (also from Hallmark): "As the years go by, we begin to learn what matters. Years don't matter. Differences don't matter. Love matters."

Mother adored the card! And there was peace between us on her ninety-fourth birthday.

Remember: when it comes to personal relationships and your career, optimism will win out over pessimism every time, even when it feels like negativity has a stranglehold over you.

When dealing with difficult circumstances, hang in there with persistence and show as much positivity as you can muster—at least for a while.

And do your best to understand what drives difficult behaviors. Luckily, there are Hallmark cards for everyone.

## OPTIMISM IS CORE TO
## INSPIRATIONAL LEADERSHIP

Through rigorous testing, Bain & Company identified the importance of optimism as a cornerstone of inspirational leadership. Optimism, or remaining resilient and positive despite challenges, is one key way that inspirational leaders are able to develop their inner resources and continue to be inspirational.

As mentioned in Chapter 2, Bain research also suggests that women's aspiration and confidence to reach senior leadership roles lag their male peers just at the point that they are making critical, long-term career decisions. Bain has also found women, compared to men, are less likely to…

▶ …feel comfortable advocating for themselves, at all levels of their career, to get an opportunity they want;

▶ …take risks, that is, make decisions with major upside or downside potential with respect to their careers;

▶ …voice a work-related opinion that others disagree with.

Optimism to pursue senior leadership roles, advocate for oneself, take risks, and share opinions are all critical behaviors to women advancing to positions of leadership.

# CHAPTER 6

# Learn, Evolve, Reinvent

CHARTING AND NAVIGATING YOUR COURSE must include the imperative for continual lifelong learning. I already described how I began my career—as an International Affairs major whose early experience was in the government. But as I progressed, and especially when I transitioned to the private sector, I acquired new subject matter and business competencies. Although I never returned to school to get an MBA, you might say that I reinvented myself.

As I mentioned earlier, transitioning from the government to the private sector is a hard proposition. The motivations and accountabilities in the government are very different from those of the private sector. In the government, you're responsible for managing to a taxpayer-funded budget, delivering a service, and establishing national policy. At least in the 1980s and 1990s, the metrics on how individual government employees were rated were pretty squishy.

In the business world, there is nothing squishy about how employees are rated. Quantifiable metrics are key for evaluating performance. Depending on your role in industry, you might be accountable for growing revenue year-over-year by a certain amount, increasing profits by specific percentages, retaining numbers of key employees, or capturing new deals from new clients at certain contract values.

I began my business career in the Business Development field and eventually became a Business Unit General Manager and, ultimately, a Sector President. The latter two jobs were major P&L (profit and loss) responsibilities over highly technical pieces of business.

Because business was a whole new world for me, I went on the offense to get as much new training as I could. I did this over time through a variety of means: short courses in business offered by some of the top business schools in the country, internal classes offered by the company (e.g., Capture Management and the Fundamentals of Finance), and good old-fashioned rotational assignments and on-the-job-training to expose me to different parts of the business.

Truthfully, while some of this training was welcome, some was a real slog. Rotational assignments sound good (and in retrospect were good) but at the time they occurred, the company was going through continual reorganizations, which meant that I frequently left one position and accepted another sooner than I would have preferred.

(Do frequent reorganizations sound familiar to you?)

My big break came when I was about two years into my SAIC tenure. Ken Dahlberg, SAIC's new CEO at the time, recently joined the company from General Dynamics Corporation, a major aerospace and defense firm. Ken was accustomed—as are most senior executives in the business world—to reviewing strategic plans for the business. He expected each sector not only to have an approved annual operating plan, but also a five-year projection of where we intended to go. And he wanted to be briefed on these strategic plans in short order.

I remember the direction to create strategic plans hitting SAIC like a ton of bricks.

Up to this point, we had nothing approaching a five-year plan. Though I had no previous experience in strategic planning, I volunteered willingly to take on the assignment.

My sector, which was new to me at the time, specialized in command, control, and communications systems (C3) for government customers. C3 typically involves technology and approaches to allow decision makers to make sense of data, execute decisions based on data and then communicate those decisions to others in a protected way.

Pretty hard stuff to internalize for an International Affairs major, but I was determined to give it my all.

The first thing I did was to consult with my counterparts across the company to see how they intended to create their strategic plan presentations. I found that most intended to dive deeply into the technical aspects of the engineering work they hoped to pursue.

The second thing I did was to research what good strategic plans in business look like. This research included talking with some of my mentors and others in my network who had experience in this realm.

Spoiler alert: Good strategic plans tend not to focus predominantly on deep dive technical reviews.

The third thing I did was to assemble a working group from across our sector comprised of people with different skills—everything from technical expertise to finance to business development to mergers and acquisitions.

Over the course of the next month, I became a sponge for soaking up knowledge about the C3 government market, key customers, competitors, opportunities on the horizon, possible acquisition targets, and technology trends. From this, I created a presentation focused on five-year growth and profitability goals, linked to the market and competitive landscape we envisioned. I also proposed some acquisition and technology investment ideas that the team felt would jumpstart or accelerate the effort.

When the presentation was complete, I attempted to hand the whole thing over to a Command and Control expert to brief the proposal to the CEO.

By way of background, I had a strong fear of public speaking for many years. Over time, I learned to polish my verbal communications skills and overcome anxiety in public settings (more about the power of communication in Chapter 8), but I was not fully there by the time of this important C3 presentation. Moreover, an even bigger concern was that I would not be able to handle what could become a highly technical discussion about command and control systems.

Fortunately, the team prevailed upon me to do the briefing, so I forged ahead. As it turned out, the brief was not to the CEO alone, but to the entire senior leadership team. There were seven strategic plans presented that day. I was number four. I remember sitting through the first three presentations nervously—all were far more technical than mine, delivered by seasoned engineers and scientists. Ditto the three that came after me.

After the presentations concluded, I was crestfallen but soon thereafter, amazing things started happening for me.

It turned out the CEO was most impressed with my presentation because it talked less about the technical intricacies of command and control systems and more about how we would grow the C3 business profitably. Within six months, when the Business Unit Manager of the $500 million-dollar Command and Control Unit retired, the CEO selected me to be his replacement. I am convinced that the strategic plan work, the flair for building business, and my presentation skills helped me get this job. The purpose driven work to protect our troops from roadside bombs (described in Chapter 3) was the highlight of my time as the Business Unit General Manager of this unit.

From that day forward, my work at SAIC focused principally on translating what the company's highly technical capabilities could do to help solve our customers' toughest mission problems. It was all about selling, customer satisfaction, program excellence, and pulling the levers of business to make a profit and maximize cash.

In the ensuing years, I would come up against multiple operational challenges in business I had never encountered before. And although I still was not a technical person, I mastered enough of the substance to be able to synthesize and explain to customers what was in it for them. I did not have a business degree; however, I ultimately became responsible for a significant piece of SAIC's business.

You might say I totally reinvented myself!

I had gone from one who struggled in the transition from government to the private sector, to one who was now leading a major business within a Fortune 500 company.

And that reinvention continues to this day.

Having worked for more than three decades on a full-time basis, today I have multiple part-time jobs rather than a single full-time job.

In addition to serving as a Special Advisor to Bain & Company, the other pillar of my new focus is serving on corporate and non-profit boards.

Serving on boards is not like being in the top management of a company or government organization. Hence the need for reinvention and continual learning on my part.

Whereas the role of management is to run the organization, the role of the board is to oversee the strategy, governance, talent, and execution within the organization. Boards of Directors are usually comprised of highly experienced people who are used to being in charge and calling the shots on a daily basis.

But that is not the role of the Board.

Rather, the Board meets periodically to perform certain governance duties according to law and/or the bylaws of the organization. Among the top duties of the Board are: oversight of company strategy, approval of the annual operating plan, hiring, firing, and establishing compensation for top management and reviewing risk.

I had been exposed to all of these tasks, at least on a general basis, but I had always been on the management side.

So I needed to master the skill of learning to step back, not manage as though I were the President or CEO and ask the right questions to spur discussion and ensure that multiple approaches were considered.

How did I learn all this and actually land several board positions? By doing what I always do: I consulted with mentors and members of my network with experience in corporate board work, researched the role and responsibilities of boards (through an organization called the National Association of Corporate Directors—NACD), and practiced my "elevator speech" on the value I could bring (and what I would hope to get) from Board service. I also did my homework big time on the market and company dynamics of each board with which I was interviewing.

I now serve on two public and three private boards. Each does business with the US government, which means that my knowledge of the government market and my operational experience at SAIC have given me a running start in assisting these companies. I don't prescribe solutions, but rather try to ask the right questions. Again, that is in keeping with the role of the Board, and it's a good start.

But good starts are not enough. I recognize that I need to continue growing in this new role.

That's why I continue to take courses at NACD and why I still look for mentors (including my B2B women's group) to give me advice and feedback.

Bottom line—if your knowledge base remains stagnant, so will you. So go on the offense when it comes to new learning. Never stop expanding your base of knowledge.

Learn, evolve, reinvent.

## WHERE ARE THE WOMEN ON BOARDS?

When it comes to Women in the Boardroom, numerous studies have found that female leadership correlates with better corporate governance and financial performance. However, women leaders remain underrepresented. According to a study authored by the independent research organization, MSCI:

- Out of 4,218 companies covered in the study, women held 15 percent of all directorships.

- 73.5 percent of companies have at least one female director, though that number drops to just 20.1 percent for boards with at least three women. Academic research suggests that three women may constitute a critical mass to allow women to contribute more equally to group decision making.

- Companies that had strong female leadership generated a Return on Equity of 10.1 percent per year versus 7.4 percent for those without (on an equal-weighted basis).

- Companies lacking board diversity tend to suffer more governance-related controversies than average.

# CHAPTER 7

# Lead a Full Life Beyond Work

FINDING JOY AND FULFILLMENT OUTSIDE OF WORK has been just as important to me as having purposeful work.

Thinking back to Chapter 3—"Be Part of Something Big"—I talked about pursuing a purpose-driven career and a purpose-driven private life. In fact, I would argue, this is not only possible, but it should be encouraged. A well-balanced individual, one who devotes time to family, friends, and outside pursuits, will be much happier and more productive than one who strives to achieve work accomplishments alone. If you are a leader, you should make it clear to your team that going home at a reasonable hour (as well as taking regular vacations) is not only a good thing, but an essential thing.

From my earliest years, I always knew I wanted children—never even crossed my mind that I needed to choose between family and career—so, unlike many women of my generation, I took the plunge into motherhood in my twenties. My children became the purpose that drove my private life.

By the age of twenty-seven, I was working at the House Armed Services Committee and was a mom to both Sam, born in 1984 and Regina, born in 1986. The committee granted me seven weeks of maternity leave after the birth of each child (which was really five weeks of maternity leave plus two weeks of annual leave I had accrued). In the mid-1980s, there had been no other professional women on the Committee staff who had given birth, so they literally had to make up a policy to cover me.

Today's maternity benefits are more generous in some cases, but not all. For example, if you work for a large organization today, you are covered by the Family and Medical Leave Act, which guarantees up to twelve weeks of <u>unpaid</u> leave for those who need time to deal with certain family and health issues, including childbirth. Smaller employers, however, are not bound by this legislation. In addition, when it comes to being paid while on maternity leave, MomsRising.org reports that only 13 percent of Americans have access to <u>paid</u> family leave through their employer and only 37 percent have personal <u>paid</u> leave. I'm proud that during my tenure as Secretary of the Air Force, we increased the amount of maternity and paternity leave for members of the armed forces because we believed that we needed to become a more flexible employer, especially to retain more high-quality women. You'll read more about this in Chapter 15.

In my case, I was able to make seven weeks work, and I returned to the committee, ready to establish my rhythm as a working mom. It was hard at first—I was an anomaly, exhausted from lack of sleep and breast feeding. There were no such things as lactation rooms in those days, and I remember pumping breast milk in the restroom. (Thank goodness many organizations—including the Department of Defense—have advanced the ball since then to make reasonable accommodations for new mothers!)

Here's how I established my rhythm—first, on the Homefront. I consistently followed four pillars when parenting my children:

► Establish priorities

► Give the gift of time

► Invest in experiences over things

► Let go of the guilt

Let me illustrate these points with a few examples.

When my children were young, I knew working parents who performed all childcare duties by themselves, with little or no help from family, nannies, or childcare centers. Some also prepared fabulous meals on a nightly basis and took great pride in having beautifully appointed homes.

This was not me. Meals, cleaning, laundry, and doing all the childcare with no help, plus holding down a busy, full-time job, would have driven me mad. (My husband loved his children but was no help whatsoever when it came to household duties or childcare.)

So I simplified. You might even say I outsourced almost all of the household jobs. It was a matter of priorities.

First, we hired nannies over the years to stay at the house or come to the house during the workweek. These women not only cared for the children while I was at work, they also did the laundry, kept the house reasonably tidy, and put a meal on the table every night. Maggie, Ana, and Jerry were lifesavers for me on more occasions than I can recount—both when I was a married parent as well as when I was a single parent.

Did they accomplish every task exactly as I would have done it? Absolutely not. But good enough was good enough. The main thing was that the children were well cared for and, when I arrived home at night, the essentials of the household had been taken care of, and I could devote myself exclusively to the family.

I know what some of you are thinking. Not everyone has the resources to be able to outsource household chores. And you are right about that.

But if you intend to work outside the household, you must—at a minimum—seek quality child care, which likely means that you will need to analyze your household expenditures, and then stop or curtail certain activities in order to make room for other expenses—like child care centers, babysitters, or nannies.

And then, beyond spending time with your children and partner, you should simply consider letting go of some of the other time-consumers in your life. Keep the meals super simple. And a messy house is good enough. You will burn yourself out if you try to do it all to perfection with no help. And let's face it: fancy meals and exacting housework are not likely to help in a big way with your relationships.

What will help in your relationships is giving time—that's what my children tell me was the most valuable thing I gave to them. And in this day of constant personal device use, I mean time without constantly looking at your phone.

When I gave time as the kids were growing up, I knew what was going on with their homework and was able to help, if needed, on a daily basis. I knew their friends and their friends' parents—a big deal with teenagers. I was not only the source of discipline, but also the source of fun in our household. I spent all my spare time focused on them as they were growing up. I learned to read their moods and any changes in behavior; I could tell when they were off, depressed, or worried. Furthermore, I was always able to listen attentively (before reacting), and they were always able to talk things through with me.

After my divorce from their father, I devoted even more time. Unlike my mother, I steered my children away from any ongoing controversies between their father and me, and I arranged my schedule so that I could be home most nights.

Fortunately, though employers in those days never talked about flexibility in the workplace, I was always able to be reasonably flexible when I needed to—this is crucial for managing the work part of the work/life balance. And when I needed to, I asked for time off unapologetically. For example, I never had trouble getting time off for a medical appointment or school event—though I was careful not to ask for flexibility too frequently. Today, increasing numbers of employers recognize that more flexibility can be a powerful recruiting, retention, and engagement tool for the workforce and are leveraging flexible schedules like never before.

The third element (I swear by this one, though my children may not agree) is to invest in experiences over things.

That is, if you have a choice between purchasing designer shoes for your child or exploring a new place or activity, go with the experience over the thing.

This is easier said than done in the consumer society we live in. It may have been my own modest upbringing, but I can tell you with certainty that I held the line against what I considered to be outrageous purchases.

On the other hand, I was always willing to invest in experiences (which require giving more time) like reading before bed, playing imagination games, trips to the playground, swimming pool, and parks. As they got older, we explored the many sights of Washington, D.C. I also insisted that the three of us do some charitable activities together so that my children would realize that there were many who were not nearly as privileged as we were.

By the time Sam and Regina became teenagers, we expanded our joint experiences to include world travel. Over time (and mostly during their spring and summer breaks from high school and college) we visited the major capitals of Europe, Asia, and Africa. Sometimes it would be all three of us, sometimes just two (because one child or the other had other activities during the period), and sometimes my best friend and former Military Assistant from the 1990s, Dell, would join us.

We still laugh to this day about some of the adventures we had, the places we saw, and the people we met. I have found that family vacations (and other joint experiences) are among the top memories my children cherish most from their younger years. Sam and Regina will remember our safari in Tanzania and sunrise over the Serengeti long after designer clothes wear thin.

Now, I will admit right away—I was extremely fortunate on the child front. We avoided some of the huge pitfalls that families sometimes encounter. My children were happy, healthy, and did well in school. Fortunately, they never fell in with the wrong crowd or succumbed to alcohol or drug abuse. And I earned sufficient money—despite my divorce—to provide a very comfortable lifestyle for all of us.

Not to say parenting was without its challenges, though.

For example, when the kids were young, they bickered constantly over silly things like who would lead the way when we rode bicycles, or who would hold the kite first when we flew it on the beach. I tried the obvious solution—taking turns—but this never seemed to work well.

One approach that was successful for us was "special time," meaning that in addition to doing things all together, I made it a point to select periodic activities with one child alone. This allowed for undivided attention to that child and became "special time" that each looked forward to. They each had a say in what we did together, though certainly not every request or desire was fulfilled.

As I think back, the parenting challenge that seemed steepest to me (at the time) was when Sam, at the age of sixteen, told me that he is gay.

I immediately asked him, "Are you sure?" He told me that he was, that he had felt different for years and only now felt comfortable enough to tell me. I reassured him that I loved him no matter what, and I was grateful that he took me into his confidence. We made plans to tell his sister and stepfather; and I strongly urged that he wait until college to tell others.

You see, I was desperate to have others be equally supportive of him, and I was not sure that his high school community would be welcoming. At that time, there were no other "out" students at his school.

Sam disagreed. Not only was he determined to come out, he committed to starting a new organization at school—a Gay Straight Alliance—to serve as a social club and a platform to raise awareness.

And this is precisely what he did.

I was floored by all this and convinced that it would go badly. But Sam's mind was made up, so I braced myself for what would come next.

As it turned out, the student population took the news extremely well. In fact, it was not nearly the big deal I thought it might be. Sam ended up with even more friends. He launched the Gay Straight Alliance and became more of a leader at school than he was before. When it came time to apply to college, this entire experience became the subject of his college essay. The University of Pennsylvania granted him early admission!

Today, Sam and Regina (who also attended top-notch schools and excelled at everything she put her mind to) are the best of friends, which is a great comfort to me. And I remain very close with both of them. We communicate regularly by phone and text. They consult me on (I believe) most, if not all, of their professional challenges and at least some of their personal challenges. When I married Frank in 2013, Sam gave me away. And when Regina married my son-in-law, Colin, in 2015, she asked me to walk her down the aisle.

We remain a tight-knit family team. They don't always follow my advice, but they do respect my opinions. And I respect theirs.

In fact, Regina was instrumental in convincing me to accept the offer to become the Secretary of the Air Force. When I finally shared with my children that this opportunity had come my way—but I was hesitant to accept—Regina called me out on it.

"What do you mean you're not sure about taking the job?" she said. "How can you not accept? You have been preparing your entire professional life for this moment. And think about all the people you can help if you take this job. You have already done everything for Sam and me—we are launched—now you need to do this for you and for the military."

Out of the mouths of babes! And she was right. I never looked back after that.

So far, Sam, Regina, and I have not yet missed a Thanksgiving or Christmas together. Realistically, I know this will end someday—but I cherish these times together and look forward to the day that some little person calls me Grandma.

For then, I will have the chance to focus on priorities, time, and experience with the next generation!

As a fifteen-year empty-nester, my life no longer revolves around Sam and Regina on a daily basis. My husband, Frank, and I are now avid boaters and have found a whole new group of friends at the marina where we keep the boat. We also recently began something called "kidnap weekends." The idea here is to block off two three-day weekends each year, with each of us accepting responsibility for planning one surprise weekend for the other. It can be anything you think the other would enjoy—the element of surprise is what makes it super fun and hopefully romantic.

And I make it a point to block more "me" time as well—for pleasure reading, exercise, and reconnecting with the friends I've made throughout my lifetime. I also get more sleep!

The point of the story is this: having a full life outside of work has been a big part of who I am. There is no question that I am a happier person because of it, despite the zig-zags of troubled marriages and the inevitable challenges of raising children.

It pains me when I sometimes hear millennial women talk about how they can't have it all—career and family—because they feel guilty about not being able to give 100 percent to both endeavors.

My daughter and some of her friends have educated me about the phenomenon of millennial guilt. All of these women in their early thirties have friends who feel continual guilt about the decisions and tradeoffs they must make.

"How can we give our best to our children if we are not home full-time? How will we find time for our partners and friends? How will I excel at work now that I have a family?" Millennial anxiety around work/life balance issues seems even more extreme than the guilt my generation experienced.

Research from the Baby Center, an online media company that provides information on conception, pregnancy, birth, and early childhood development, provides context about this constant anxiety. A telling statistic is that after childbirth, modern mothers report adding more than nine hours on average to their schedules. It's a classic case of more to do and not enough time to get everything done, so I can understand why this seems like a hard tradeoff for so many!

Here's what I tell them: Even though social media may lead you to believe otherwise, no one is 100 percent perfect, effective, or happy all the time—either personally or professionally. Perfection is not real life. Balance is real life. And you can get there if, first and foremost, you let go of the guilt.

After all, when it comes to raising children, study after study has demonstrated that children grow up and prosper just as well in high-quality childcare environments as they do with a loving and stable, stay-at-home parent. So if you have ambitions beyond raising a family, don't repress those desires, go for it!

I also feel strongly that if you want (and can afford) to stay home with your children for an extended period, you should go for that too.

There is no right or wrong answer here; working outside the home, working as a stay-at-home mom, or being a "mompreneur" (a mom who pursues a home-based career) are individual choices. My point is that while it's okay to be driven by your personal economic, career, and family ambitions, you should not be driven by guilt.

On the professional front, if your boss or organization cannot accommodate your need for flexibility or if the team falls apart if you are absent periodically for family reasons, you should probably start looking for a new boss, employer, or team. And on the home front, if your childcare arrangement is so inflexible that occasional changes in schedule cannot be accommodated, you need to seek alternative or supplemental childcare arrangements. Don't feel guilty! And if you simplify the non-essential chores, you can beat the additional nine-hour statistic cited by the Baby Center.

Here's the bottom line: There are times when you will need to double down for a work project and other times when you will need to focus on family. Don't apologize or fret over this; work to surround yourself—in both the workplace and home-front—with people and structures that can support you in this balance.

I say again: you absolutely can have a successful career and family life—if you want to.

▸ Make your priorities and stick with them. Don't expect to be perfect at everything all the time.

▸ Don't try to do everything by yourself. Surround yourself with those who will help you balance.

▸ The biggest gift you can give is your high-quality time—put the devices away.

▸ Prioritize experiences over things.

▸ Let go of the guilt.

And keep in mind the other strategies discussed throughout this book. Continuous learning, persistence, positivity, and doing the Zig-Zag, among others, have served me well in my private life just as they have in my career.

## THE VALUE OF FLEXIBLE WORK
## AND HOME ENVIRONMENTS

Bain & Company's research has found that mid-career women are 61 percent more likely to have a spouse with an equally or more intense job and six times more likely to be the primary caregiver for couples with a child/children. These dynamics highlight the importance and value of formal and informal flexible working options for all employees, and especially women.

One metric of how well a company is meeting the needs of those who work for them is employee Net Promoter Score, a methodology developed by Bain to measure employee loyalty, based on their willingness to recommend their employer as a place to work. Bain found, in conjunction with the Australian Chief Executive Women group, that companies where flexible arrangements are widely used have an employee Net Promoter Score 60 percentage points higher than those without any flexible options. The same research also found that employees of companies where flexible arrangements are widely used rated their company 72 percentage points higher as a place where women can progress to senior levels as compared to employees of companies without flexible working options.

Flexibility at home is important too. In *Lean In. Women, Work, and the Will to Lead*, Sheryl Sandberg writes about the importance of making your partner your real partner. Today, most women still perform the majority of childrearing and household duties; yet couples who share responsibilities on a more equal basis are stronger—and their children benefit from seeing their parents model equality.

PART 2

# LEAD AND INSPIRE TEAMS

# CHAPTER 8

# Speak Up
# and Listen Deeply

UNDERSTANDING HOW TO INSPIRE AND LEAD people has been a big part of my leadership journey in both the government and business sectors. Becoming an effective communicator is an absolute must the higher up the leadership chain you go.

Effective communication involves everything from clear, concise, and persuasive writing to effective oral communication—whether it's speaking with your small team or before a public audience of thousands of people. Many people forget—but I learned the hard way—that at least 50 percent of communication is active listening and making best efforts to understand where your team or listeners are coming from (emotional intelligence). Communication comes naturally to some, but it didn't for me.

This chapter focusses primarily on polishing public speaking skills before a large audience—something every professional needs to grow comfortable with if you are to advance to a senior, visible role—and communications tips for rallying smaller teams.

My first major experiences in public speaking and leading a team were pretty scary, but I eventually mastered key skills and learned that I could do it. And you can too.

Though I always have thought of myself as being a good conversationalist one-on-one, I had zero experience in public speaking or public presentations during my first twelve years working for the Army and for the House Armed Services Committee. I never needed to and never particularly wanted to, which meant I was sorely lacking in some very important communication skills.

As an individual contributor, and one of the junior ones at that, there was always someone superior to me who would deliver the briefing—and I was happy with that. The truth is, public speaking terrified me.

Terrified or not, I took a crash course in public speaking in 1992, at the age of thirty-three.

At this juncture, the Presidential race was on between President George H. W. Bush and Governor Bill Clinton. My boss, Congressman Les Aspin, Chairman of the House Armed Services Committee, was a defense advisor to Governor Clinton, who, at the time, was not considered to be well-versed in matters of national defense. I was sent to Salt Lake City, Utah, to deliver a speech that Aspin had been invited to do; however, he was busy, and the task fell to me. Meanwhile, both President Bush and Governor Clinton had been invited to address this same conference—the National Guard Association—but both sent word that they were otherwise engaged.

As I flew out to Salt Lake City and began to agonize over my speech, my only consolation was that the conference was shaping up to be a sleepy one. Over the next twenty-four hours, I wrote, revised, crumpled up, and started my speech over and over again. With each new draft, I felt the churnings in my stomach and the pure anxiety pulsing through my veins. I literally pulled an all-nighter the day before the speech and practiced it many times in front of the mirror.

By morning, I seriously considered calling the conference organizers to tell them I was sick (by the way, I really was sick by this time), but the fear of being fired held me back.

Sleepy conference or not, there were more than four thousand people in attendance when I took to the podium. I got through it—literally—by pretending to be an actress in a play (thereby psychologically separating myself from something that might have been a fiasco)! As a confident actress, I smiled, waved to the crowd and launched into my speech, which, by the way, was familiar territory to me because I had worked the issues I was discussing as part of my beat on the committee staff. And having practiced the words all night, I pretty much had the text memorized.

Much to my amazement, the crowd listened intently, applauded frequently, laughed at the right times, and gave me a standing ovation when the speech concluded. The actress thing had worked! (It took me years to gain the perspective that the real thing that worked was preparation, though the actress thing was a useful crutch at the time!)

No sooner did I step off the stage than I was surrounded by a number of participants who complimented me on my remarks. A number of people even said I was inspirational.

Inspirational? Me?

At this point, I was handed an extraordinary message: Both President Bush and Governor Clinton had reversed themselves and the two were now headed to Salt Lake City to address the National Guard Association. Because this was a sudden decision and Clinton had no advance people on the ground, I became deputized as his advance agent for the next two days (a major learning experience in and of itself). Les Aspin flew out as well, and together we briefed Governor Clinton on the state of play at the conference. Les Aspin let me do most of the talking, and I did so with confidence—no acting needed this time.

The Clinton speechwriter was present during the briefing and had the task of incorporating major National Guard-related points into the already drafted speech. The bulk of the speech (I was told) was written with the idea of countering what they thought President Bush would say.

By the next morning, I was exhausted but eager to hear how the President's and Governor Clinton's speeches would play out. All the smart campaign people believed that President Bush would use this opportunity to attack Governor Clinton for "dodging" the Vietnam draft; Clinton's remarks contained a detailed rebuttal to this argument.

Never underestimate your ability to predict the future wrong.

Les Aspin and I were in the front row when President Bush arrived in the hall. Surrounded by Secret Service agents, he approached the stage to thunderous applause. Les Aspin and I were in the front row and heard his every word.

And not a single word related to Clinton and "dodging" the draft. This meant that the entirety of Clinton's speech had to be rewritten in very short order.

When President Bush concluded his remarks and departed, Aspin and I were ushered back to the holding area for Clinton. Staffers were racing around in near panic as they attempted to rewrite his remarks and feed new words into the teleprompter. Clinton was at center stage, quietly watching the chaos surrounding him. All of a sudden, he shouted, "Enough! Everyone out! I need quiet time to collect my thoughts." With that, everyone filed out of the room and we took our seats.

As if all this confusion was not enough, no sooner did Clinton take to the stage and begin to speak than there was a power outage in the hall, plunging everyone into darkness. The conference organizers somehow rigged up a substitute microphone and brought candles to the podium, but the teleprompter was useless.

Much to my amazement, Clinton appeared unfazed. He made a joke about the lights and brought a light-hearted touch to the gathering. He thanked those in attendance and remembered all the names of the dignitaries on stage. He gave a cogent national defense speech with three or four main points, including my specific suggestions relating to the National Guard, and his personal experience with the Arkansas National Guard as Governor. I found his comments to be inspirational, especially his personal stories about how the Arkansas National Guard saved lives and how proud he was to be associated with them.

And he delivered the entire speech without a single written note.

Flash forward: Clinton won the election, Les Aspin became the first Secretary of Defense under President Clinton, and I became Assistant Secretary of Defense for Reserve Affairs, which is the top policy adviser to the Secretary of Defense on all matters pertaining to—wait for it—the National Guard and Reserve. For five years, I advocated for the 1.8 million part-time military members, their personnel policies, training, and equipping.

To be sure, the speech in Salt Lake City and the impromptu advance work for the Clinton campaign, by themselves, did not get me this important new job, but these events did provide me with important visibility. Salt Lake City demonstrated that I could be a persuasive and polished verbal communicator, an important attribute for anyone rising up through the leadership ranks. Additionally, coming through in a pinch is another important attribute.

Over time, I delivered many more speeches and learned some important tips to make it easier on myself. President Clinton was a master at this. For example:

▶ Keep it simple. Convey three or four main points in a speech. Your audience will not retain much more than that.

▶ Include stories to convey your points. Stories are far more memorable than data and statistics alone. Personal stories are the best of all.

▶ Demonstrate to the audience that you care—and mean it! Authenticity and passion for your subject go a long way.

▶ Humor can be great—or it can be disastrous. I find the best and safest humor is self-deprecation.

▶ Practice helps delivery every single time.

▶ Finally, don't be afraid to repeat. I am sure that Governor Clinton was able to gracefully recover from the failed tele-prompter and deliver a terrific speech because he had given the same basic speech before. He simply needed to tailor it a bit for the National Guard.

Years later, after establishing the mentoring program for high potentials in my Business Unit at SAIC, several of our mentees revealed that they, too, were struggling with public speaking. I knew just what to advise them.

SAIC sponsored participation in an organization called Toast-masters International, a non-profit headquartered in Colorado but with more than sixteen thousand "clubs" all over the world.

At Toastmasters, participants overcome their fear of public speaking by actually doing. They practice different types of speeches in front of other club members who then provide feed-back on how to improve.

I received very positive feedback about the organization from the SAICers who participated. And let's face it, joining an organization like Toastmasters is way more fun than staying up all night and practicing in front of the mirror!

My other key learning about communication—how to communicate effectively and persuasively with teams—came early in my tenure as the Assistant Secretary of Defense for Reserve Affairs.

You must understand—when I took the Reserve Affairs assignment, I catapulted overnight from being an individual contributor on Capitol Hill to being the leader of more than 120 people on my immediate staff.

This was when I learned that when it comes to leading people, listening deeply and broadly is crucial. Getting to know your people as people is important, too, because it shows that you care. This means not only listening to the verbal word, but also to the non-verbal signals that offer clues into what people are thinking and feeling. When you listen deeply to the verbal and non-verbal and get to know your team as real human beings, not only will you receive good factual input, you will also come to understand and empathize more with the professional and personal challenges your team faces. And you will be a better leader for it!

Let me offer an example.

As the newly-confirmed Assistant Secretary, I remember my first staff meeting with the Reserve Affairs team vividly.

I walked down the corridor from my office to the conference room that first Monday morning, sat down, and looked at my new team—comprised at that time of older career civilians and military personnel (I was only thirty-four at the time). Although I was super nervous and self-conscious about my youth, I also sensed that all of them were genuinely anxious to meet and get to know me.

So what did I do?

Without any personal introduction, I began to talk from my prepared script. I laid out a vision for the future about how we would use the part time National Guard and Reserve forces differently than the past. Basically, I was pitching the policy then Chairman Aspin (and now Secretary of Defense Aspin) called for and that I had spoken about in Salt Lake City. The approach called for blocking the most serious proposed cuts to the Army National Guard, improving readiness of these part-time forces and then using them more regularly in day-to-day military missions, not just in the event World War III broke out.

Basically, I talked.

And talked.

And talked.

After telling everyone exactly what we were going to do, I gave direction on some specific tactical ideas (without specifying who would take the lead for anything) and said we would discuss progress at our next Monday morning staff meeting.

"Any questions?" I asked.

There were none.

"Great! See you next week," I said.

By the time we assembled the following Monday, I was excited to receive reports about how much work the team had produced. I sat down and suggested that we go around the room and offer individual comments. It fell to the person on my right to begin.

He looked at me like I had three heads and appeared to have no idea what I was talking about.

Looking back on this, I handled these two meetings pretty much all wrong. Although it was good that I brought the beginnings of a vision to the table, I should not have commandeered the entire meeting with specific ideas and barked orders. Rather,

I should have launched this first meeting by asking each member of the team to introduce themselves and to give me some of their background. I should have done the same for them.

This did not occur to me at the time—I was trying so hard to be business-like, and I assumed that all of us had read each other's bios—but I now know that getting to know people as people is a really important part of leadership. So is valuing the experience, opinions, and input of the team that surrounds you.

After the second staff meeting, I was lucky that the older and much more experienced senior civilian who led the team while I was awaiting Senate confirmation filled me in on a few things.

First, he gently told me that one of my ideas (at least as I had presented it at the first meeting) was not workable—it had been tried before and failed. However, perhaps an alternative could be found. He suggested that I seek the thoughts and reactions from others around the table on how we might accomplish the overall goal, but in a different way.

He also recommended that I make clear who was responsible for what at the conclusion of the meeting—not simply leave follow up as a generalized matter with no one in particular responsible. And there needed to be reasonable buy-in from the staff about timelines and the overall way forward. Finally, he told me that one of the staff members was struggling due to family matters. It was a hard time for her. She needed some space, so it would be best if she did not lead the project, but rather supported it, at that time.

I think I did much better by the third Monday morning. I began the meeting by telling everyone a little bit about my first few weeks on the job and about myself. I explained that I was trying to come up to speed quickly and struggling to settle into my new responsibilities at the Pentagon. I also explained that I was juggling some things at home, like figuring out a new car-pooling arrangement for my two young children now that I could no longer share regularly in the school drop-off and pick-up schedules. (There were a few sympathetic nods and smiles around the table about this one.)

I emphasized to everyone that I was committed to being the best advocate possible for our men and women in the National Guard and Reserve but that I needed their help, support and best thinking to overcome some of the challenges that we would be facing. Budgets were tight and severe cuts were looming unless we could turn the situation around.

Then I asked that we go around the table so that everyone could tell me something about himself or herself. I apologized that I did not do this at our first gathering. Better late than never.

After that, we began brainstorming some of the issues. For the most part, I sat back and listened.

Over time, the Reserve Affairs team—plus a few terrific political appointees who joined us within the first year—built a series of initiatives that fell within the overall vision I brought to the table on Day 1. My top job became selling and defending these initiatives within the halls of the Pentagon and on Capitol Hill.

Over the next five years, not only did we ultimately block the most severe cuts, but we also enhanced the readiness of some units within the National Guard and Reserve, we began using these forces on a more routine basis for important national missions, and we regularized many of the benefits (with those of the active duty forces) to protect members and their families.

And so, I began to learn that communication, including deep listening (verbal and non-verbal), getting to know people as people, and sharing some of myself with authenticity and sincerity were essential techniques for leading and inspiring teams.

I also have come to believe that these same communication skills, coupled with my strong focus on people, ethics, and teamwork (See Chapters 9, 10, and 11) allowed me to beat the odds and largely overcome a particularly insidious form of gender bias—something Sheryl Sandberg called the "likeability penalty" in *Lean In*. This "penalty" explains why many successful women are viewed as overly aggressive "bitches" whereas equally successful men who exhibit the same leadership behaviors are viewed as strong and likeable leaders.

I'm not saying that those who have worked with or for me through the years always agreed with my actions or decisions, but I do believe most felt heard, appreciated, and valued. I am generous with the praise I offer in public and careful to offer negative feedback only in private. I take genuine interest in others. And although tough decisions are always difficult for some to accept, I have found that they go down better with a team if there is a foundation of mutual trust.

Wouldn't it be great if trust could be forged in an instant? Well it can't. Trust must be earned over time. And for this, you will need to communicate effectively.

## COMMUNICATION SKILLS
## ARE PAYING DIVIDENDS FOR WOMEN

Compared to men, women exhibit higher emotional intelligence, are more effective at communication, and display a democratic leadership style.

The Korn Ferry Hay Group used data from 55,000 professionals in ninety countries and found that women scored higher than men did on nearly all emotional intelligence competencies. Because women are more emotionally intelligent, they are better at listening and communication.

A New York Times article cites research that found women interrupt less (but are interrupted more), pay closer attention to other people's nonverbal cues, and use a more democratic leadership style compared with men's more autocratic style. The result is that women build coalitions and reach consensus more quickly. Women's participation-driven communication style translates into a more democratic leadership style.

According to Alice Eagly, a professor at Northwestern University, female leaders, on average, are more democratic and participative than male leaders. John Gastil, a professor at University of Washington, notes that democratic leaders distribute responsibility among the membership, empower group members, and aid the group's decision-making process.

However, a Northern Kentucky University study observed that although subjects rated, on average, participative (democratic) leaders to be 16 percent more effective and 34 percent more preferred than authoritarian ones, male leaders were rated as 21 percent more effective and 12 percent more preferred to female leaders. Unfortunately, women continue to face gender stereotypes and bias.

# CHAPTER 9

# Role Model Ethical Behavior

REMEMBER I SAID EMBRACE CHANGE with persistence and posi-tivity—at least for a while? There is one glaring exception to this rule. Don't ever embrace and stick with a new set of circumstances if it involves unethical behavior.

Ethics is both an individual and a team sport. By this, I mean that each of us is charged with doing the right thing individually, even when it's hard and even when no one is looking. Likewise, each of us is charged to report if others within our environments fail to act ethically. A few bad apples can bring down the very best of organizations.

Having been exposed to many people in government and busi-ness with authority and power, I have found that, all too often, leaders become intoxicated with their sense of entitlement. This causes some people to think they can get away with inappropri-ate and unethical behavior, which is pretty stupid, because people with greater authority, position, and power tend to be watched and scrutinized more closely by everyone around them.

Nowadays, the public or employees of an organization expect—and I believe increasingly demand—those with power and authority to act ethically. People want to see their leaders be role models for the behavior they expect from others. Those that say one thing and act a different way are far less likely to get away with it these days. That's because more and more people feel empowered to film, record, document, or otherwise report abuse or ethical violations.

Years ago, long before social media, the media treated the private lives of politicians and captains of industry as out-of-bounds for reporting. Years ago, a conversation in a private setting largely remained private. Years ago, affairs in the office environment were whispered about but no action was taken. Years ago, there was little or no recourse against abusive behaviors on airlines or in department stores.

No more.

Today, whether it's the #MeToo movement bringing down famous and powerful men, or the traditional media relentlessly reporting on the alleged financial and sexual entanglements of President Trump, or the company hotline through which an employee can report anonymously about misbehavior on the part of a senior business executive, or cell-phone filming of airline employee's abuse of passengers, ethics is more of a team sport than ever before. It's not enough to simply do the right thing yourself. Rather, if someone sees something amiss in the environment, people are increasingly urged (and are finding the courage) to speak up and do something about it.

The repercussions for violating ethics can be swift and hard. One of my roles at SAIC gave me a front row seat about how critical ethical issues—and crisis communications—should be handled.

After five years leading the Command and Control unit at SAIC, I was promoted to be the Executive Vice President for Communications and Government Affairs. This job elevated me to the most senior levels of SAIC, and I regularly attended meetings with the Board of Directors. The role returned me to the familiar territory of working with the Congress and Executive branch to represent the company and to handle communications with employees, the press, and customers.

This assignment also brought home to me what happens when ethical values fail and how effective communications are essential throughout a crisis. Both the refresher in ethics and the crisis communication pieces would serve me well in the future, especially as Secretary of the Air Force.

In 2010, SAIC was performing on a time and attendance IT program for the City of New York, known as City Time. It produced steady revenue and good profitability for the company; client assessments revealed that the City was happy with SAIC performance, and all seemed to be on track.

There was one wrinkle in City Time: the program manager, Gerard Denault, was well known within the company as being difficult. He was arrogant, refused to attend staff meetings like the rest of us, insisted upon being a direct report to the Group President (though program managers of individual programs typically reported to a different boss), and he was nasty to his people. He also cut corners on what might sound like trivial ethical matters (for example, he flaunted the no-smoking policy and smoked in the office). In short, he was a jerk.

But he was a profitable jerk, and one the customer liked, so everyone put up with him.

That turned out to be a big mistake.

Thanks to a whistleblower within the company—someone who decided they simply would not put up with a hostile work environment any longer and who suspected that Gerard might be taking kickbacks from subcontractors—it was discovered that Gerard and several others had engaged in a major corruption scheme, skimming money from both the City of New York and SAIC for his (and his accomplices') private gain.

Managing the City Time scandal became the top job of every senior leader at SAIC. Ultimately, senior executives were fired, compliance programs were changed, the company paid a $500-million-dollar fine to settle the case, and Gerard, plus several others, were sentenced to twenty years in prison.

My role during the City Time scandal was to help the company manage the communications and government affairs piece. Working closely with the General Counsel, the CEO, and the Board of Directors, I urged that we not hunker down and simply allow the lawyers to work alone behind closed doors. Rather, I urged that we tell employees, customers, the press, and Congress: what we knew, what we did not yet know, and how we intended to follow up. We emphasized that we would fully cooperate with the investigating authorities and that we would provide periodic updates as we learned more.

City Time was a bad experience—it demonstrated how much damage a few unethical people could do to an otherwise terrific organization.

City Time also taught me not to put up with jerks. Someone who is willing to play fast and loose with small rules may well violate extremely serious rules as well.

Finally, City Time reinforced for me that ethics is a team sport; everyone in an organization has the obligation to speak up if they see something wrong.

Although the City of New York is unlikely ever to hire SAIC again for a major job, I am happy to report that the company did not lose other customers, nor was it called before Congress as a result of the City Time reputational hit. In part, this was due to the company's acceptance of responsibility and proactive crisis communications.

Another lesson learned in ethics: While serving in the 1990s as the Assistant Secretary of Reserve Affairs, I watched as multiple senior government officials got into enormous trouble by using military air travel for trips that could have been easily accomplished through commercial travel—and at much less expense to the taxpayer. Unauthorized military air, private charters, expensive office renovations, accepting favors from lobbyists or otherwise wasting taxpayer dollars should be an obvious "no-no" to all who work in the government (wasting shareholder money in private companies also is an obvious "no-no"). Yet repeatedly, those in power commit such acts and think they will get away with it.

Today's headlines are replete with examples.

Former Secretary of Health and Human Services, Tom Price, was fired by President Trump for taking more than two dozen private flights at taxpayer expense.

Former Environmental Protection Administrator Scott Pruitt didn't stop at expensive flights. Among other actions, he secured hefty raises for two loyal staffers even after those raises were denied by the White House; he accepted a sweetheart housing arrangement from a lobbyist; he used his government staff for personal duties including soliciting a lucrative job for his wife, and spent $43,000 of the taxpayer's money to create a soundproof telephone booth for himself at EPA headquarters so that he could conduct secure telephone calls. Scott Pruitt was also forced out of the Trump Administration, according to press reports.

Both Price and Pruitt were men in positions of authority and power. Both, no doubt, felt entitled. Both somehow felt the activity would go unnoticed. Both were wrong.

I have often told my children: at the end of the day, all you have is your own good name, the good name of your family, and the reputation of your organization.

Don't ever squander them.

Rather, be a role model for the behavior you wish to see in others. This means treat people with dignity and respect, don't cut corners on ethics, don't allow yourself to feel entitled to anything more than anyone else, follow the rules even when no one is looking, and don't be a jerk. Don't ever compromise on ethics. Period.

You will never Lead and Inspire a team to do great things if you get this one wrong.

## STRONG ETHICS MAKES GOOD BUSINESS SENSE

Not only is ethical behavior the right thing to do morally, and often legally, there are concrete financial benefits to running an ethical company. The Aveta Business Institute outlines that companies with good ethical policies earn:

- ▶ Marketing advantages over their competitors, because customers want to establish and continue their relations with the company.

- ▶ Improved employee performance, as morale is higher.

- ► Reputation management, given that a bad reputation from unethical behavior often leads to scandal, lower stock price, public scrutiny, and low employee morale.

- ► Legal and financial incentives from regulatory bodies, as well as lower costs to manage, hide, or control unethical behavior.

Laura Kray, a researcher at the Haas School of Business has found that men tend to have more lenient ethical standards than women. In a study conducted with Michael Haselhuhn, Kray found that men tend to apply ethical principles egocentrically—when the situation affects them negatively they perceive the situation as unethical, but when it benefits them, they perceive it as a gray area and more ethically flexible. In contrast, women are more likely to see ethical decisions as ethical decisions (not gray areas) and act in an ethical manner. This does not suggest all men are unethical or all women are ethical, but it highlights another advantage of diversity on a leadership team—more people who may look at a situation or set of decisions differently.

# CHAPTER 10

# Put People First

SAID IT IN MY INTRO, and I will say it again, if you get the people part of any equation right, the other parts—strategy, goals, and technology—will be more likely to follow. This is especially true during times of great change or dysfunction, because people can feel alienated or left behind. When this happens, they will resist, become negative, or even look to stop a new effort. When introducing new approaches or technologies into the work environment, it's crucial that you invest time in bringing your people along with you on the change journey.

To Lead and Inspire in a new direction, your team must feel engaged and heard. So always put people first and think through how they will be affected by a new process, policy, and organization—this is crucial!

And while Put People First sometimes means bringing entire employee populations along the journey of change, it also means ensuring that individual performers don't get lost in the processes and policies of a big organization.

I have two examples to share.

After City Time was settled, the Board and senior leaders of the company began to refocus on the business and the future of SAIC. Eventually, it was decided that the company would "spin" into two separate companies—each with a different focus area and cost structure. I was promoted to be one of two Group Presidents, responsible for $2 billion dollars in revenue and also named as the co-architect of what would be known as the new SAIC (the other piece of the company became known as Leidos). By now, I had been with SAIC for more than ten years; the other co-architect, Nazzic Keene, was brand new to SAIC.

This was a fascinating project, one in which we had the opportunity to take a clean sheet and build a new company from the bottom up. After a lot of thought and study, we recommended that the new SAIC change from a decentralized and entrepreneurial business model to one that followed a matrix management construct; namely, all employees would be grouped into either customer groups (e.g., Army, Navy, Civilian Agencies) or capability groups (e.g., software development, logistics, hardware integration). The customer groups would be charged with developing and winning new business, and then the capability teams would be matrixed in to perform the work once it was won.

It all made good sense—and other companies had followed a similar model with great success—but when we briefed the approach to the employees of SAIC, they looked at us like we had gone mad. Nazzic was new to the company so SAICers largely gave her a pass. The fire was directed at me.

"How can you do this to us?" they asked. "You have worked at SAIC for years and should know better. This will never work here."

They followed up with a multitude of questions, mostly relating to reporting authorities, how disagreements among senior managers would be settled, who would decide on pay raises and bonuses, and who would give final direction to employees.

Stated another way, SAICers wanted to know specifics about how this new construct would affect their working environments, compensation, and customer relationships.

All very reasonable questions—and we had not thought through enough of the answers. Moreover, we had not—in retrospect—invested enough time in engaging and listening to the very people who would be most affected by the changes.

Bottom Line: we went back to the drawing board to define as many of these dependencies and answer as many of their questions as we could. We used focus groups of employees to help with this effort. We also detailed all of the new process and procedure in written instructions that we refined many times before going final. In addition, we conducted many other sessions with employees over time to get them as comfortable as possible with the construct of the new SAIC.

Change management—as some would call this effort—turned out to be the hardest part of the project! Bringing people along, hearing their concerns, engaging them for input, and being willing to make adjustments to the plan turned out to be crucial for the success of the effort!

Fortunately, our efforts did not go unnoticed and financial rewards were forthcoming from Wall Street. Thanks in part to this investment in people and our new strategy for growing and increasing profitability, the stock value of the new SAIC appreciated more than 130 percent during the first five years following the spin.

And now a story on the second part of Put People First: preventing a terrific individual contributor from getting lost in a bureaucracy.

One of the most amazing people I met during my tenure as Secretary of the Air Force was Brian Williams. His story contains elements of all the strategies I have discussed so far; however, he has lived through things that most of us would find unimaginable. Brian very nearly was forced into "medical retirement" from the Air Force, which would have been a great loss. Luckily, we got the people part right in this story and retained Brian on active duty.

In the spring of 2012, then Staff Sergeant Brian Williams, a member of the security forces (similar to police in the civilian world) was on a mission outside Kandahar Airfield in Southern Afghanistan. This was his sixth deployment overseas in twelve years, which tells you something about the demands we place on today's military personnel.

Brian was accompanied by his military working dog, Carly, and was attempting to clear a known Taliban compound when he was severely injured by the blast of an improvised explosive device. Carly was unharmed, but Brian was nearly killed. He lost his left leg above the knee and suffered severe shrapnel wounds. Fifteen surgeries, five hundred rehabilitative therapy hours, and eighteen months later, he was released from the military hospital in Bethesda, Maryland. He adopted Carly as his own.

By way of background, as recently as the 1990s, a member of the military with severe injuries like Brian had nearly a 100 percent chance of being medically discharged from the military. This is no longer the case—at least, not necessarily.

In today's military, and especially because we have sustained seventeen years of continuous combat in the Middle East, there are far more wounded and injured personnel who remain on active duty if they seek to do so. Brian was in this category. After his long recovery period in the hospital, he was quoted as saying, "Yes, I lost most of my leg, but my heart and brain still work and that's all I need."

Looking to the future, Brian said he wanted to remain on active duty, eventually retiring from the Air Force at no less than a master sergeant (two ranks above what he was at the time). And for the short term, he said he wanted to run again.

As I said, being discharged because of an injury is no longer automatic; being retained on active duty is not automatic either. There is a lengthy process to work through in order to remain in the Air Force, and if an airman can no longer perform his or her primary job, another job must be identified for the individual. Not everyone who wishes to remain makes it through this process.

I first met Brian in 2015 at the Warrior Games, part of what the Air Force calls the Adaptive Sports Program. Adaptive Sports— like wheelchair basketball or seated volleyball—is one of the ways the Air Force's Wounded Warrior Program helps the injured, wounded, and ill to recover. I'm convinced that this program— and especially the Adaptive Sports component—gives a sense of purpose, comradery, and confidence to those who are struggling to rebound both physically and psychologically.

During my tenure, I was a big proponent of the Wounded Warrior Program. I doubled the budget, increased support staff by 30 percent, spread the word publicly about these airmen at every opportunity, and advocated to allow these warriors to remain on active duty to the maximum extent possible, even if it meant finding them a new assignment (and it usually did).

I cheered for Brian and other members of the Air Force Warrior team on multiple occasions. All this time, his paperwork requesting retention in the service was slowly winding its way through the Pentagon's coordination process. He was denied twice by two Physical Evaluation Boards. (As I said earlier, being retained is still not easy or automatic.) He appealed one final time to the higher-level Air Force body known as the Secretary of the Air Force Personnel Council. (Think of this as the Supreme Court for certain personnel actions.) This body was well aware of my focus on retaining as many wounded warriors as possible—and, after proper review, it overruled the Physical Evaluation Board and issued Brian notice that he could remain in service. My signature on the official notification solidified the deal.

Then came one of the most memorable moments of my life.

In May 2016, the Warrior Games were taking place at West Point, New York. As always, the different events were exciting, and the Air Force cheering section went wild when our seated volleyball team (including Brian) defeated the Special Operations Command team to win the gold.

When the awards program began, I had the honor of placing the gold medals over the heads of the competitors. When I reached Brian about midway down the line, he removed his medal and put it over my head instead.

I had no idea what was happening. Was this some kind of "protest" moment?

"Brian," I said. "What are you doing? You earned this medal. Well done!" And I put it over his head once more.

Again, he took it off and gave it back to me. "I want you to have it," he said. By now, everyone was staring at us, wondering what was going on. We were holding up the entire ceremony.

"I can't keep this," I said. "I did not earn it, but you did. Please take the medal."

Again, I put it over his head, and again, he removed it and put it over mine.

"Because of you," he said, "I am still in the Air Force. If you had not acted, I would have been kicked out by now."

I choked up at this point, with tears welling up in my eyes. This was a very emotional moment for me. And of all the gifts I have received in my life, I will treasure Brian's gold medal for as long as I live.

Today, Brian is a security forces instructor for new Air Force trainees in San Antonio, Texas. And if there was any doubt in your mind (there never was in mine), he runs regularly and attained the rank of Master Sergeant.

Looking back, I still feel unworthy to have received that medal, but I can tell you that the US Air Force and the young trainees that Brian engages, teaches, leads, and inspires are fortunate that he continues to serve.

And Brian is an important reminder for me that engaging with individuals is every bit as important as engaging with larger groups. After all, individual people can and do make an important difference in your organization each and every day.

To Lead and Inspire: Put People First, and I guarantee that you will be rewarded.

## ENGAGEMENT EQUALS
## TOTAL SHAREHOLDER RETURN

Research from Bain & Company has quantified that the best companies have more engaged and inspired employees—50 percent more inspired employees, in fact. Bain's research has further found that companies with a performance and inspiration orientation are four times more likely to be top performers on growth, profitability, and total shareholder return.

Inspiring leaders create inspired employees, and Bain has defined specific sets of traits characterizing inspirational leadership across four dimensions.

1. Leading the Team
2. Developing Inner Resources
3. Connecting with Others
4. Setting the Tone

Using this framework and related tools, organizations can help individuals develop as inspiring leaders, drawing on their own authentic traits and abilities. Inspirational leadership is not some innate quality that someone either has or does not have!

# CHAPTER 11

# Play to Your Strengths Within a Great Team

WE ALL HAVE BOTH STRENGTHS AND WEAKNESSES, varying degrees of expertise, and different life experiences and backgrounds. No single individual is smarter than the collective smarts of the total team, and no single individual excels at everything.

Some of the key factors Secretary Hagel cited for selecting me as the twenty-third Secretary of the Air Force were that I was astute enough to know what I knew, humble enough to admit what I did not know, and believed in playing to my strengths within a great team environment.

I certainly had a fantastic team within the Air Force. Our political appointees, uniformed military, and career civil servants collaborated well, and together we successfully tackled a variety of challenges (more on some of the key challenges and my approach to Get Things Done in Part III).

I have been part of other great teams too. I know one when I see one.

In a nutshell, I believe there are several hallmarks to great teams.

First, great teams are made up of people with diverse backgrounds and experiences. Everyone needs to both "give" and "get."

Second, great teams need a clear vision and shared goals about what they want or need to accomplish.

Third, great teams have enormous drive and energy. They thrive on getting results, especially in the face of difficult circumstances.

Fourth, great teams take time to celebrate successes. And they don't point fingers when setbacks and failures occur.

Fifth, great teams are passionate about their work and about each other—at least, most of the time.

By 1991, I had been on the staff of the House Armed Services Committee for eight years. My assignment up until that point primarily had been related to the Military Personnel and Compensation Subcommittee—and I was looking for a change.

Meanwhile, the Chairman of the Committee, Les Aspin, who was considered to be among the top Democratic defense intellectuals of the day, had a "near-death" political experience and lost the chairmanship of the committee for about two weeks. As it turned out, many of Aspin's Democratic colleagues, who were called every two years to vote on who would be committee chairs for the next Congress, felt slighted by Aspin. Many believed that they had commitments from Aspin to do something—like put a provision in the annual defense bill, or visit their districts, or help with fundraising—but that Aspin would end up welching on the deal. So when the time came to vote, the Democrats in the House voted "no" on Les Aspin.

Aspin was horrified and set out to mend fences. From his perspective, he had never gone back on his word—rather, all of these complaints were misunderstandings. He swore up and down to his colleagues that he would do better. When the next round of voting occurred two weeks later, Aspin survived and was reelected Chairman. The Democrats in the House were willing to give him one last chance.

Enter the Member Services Team (MST), a new group within the House Armed Services Committee staff that Aspin set up in the wake of his problems with the Democratic caucus. Aspin hired a veteran political operative, Larry Smith, to lead the team. (Larry, with previous experience in the Senate and in presidential campaigns, turned out to be another great mentor in my life.)

Larry envisioned the MST to be a small, diverse group that could serve as liaison between Aspin and other members to avoid future misunderstandings that potentially could cost Aspin the chairmanship in a future Congress. Though brilliant on defense, Aspin was not really a "people person" and was sloppy about keeping track of commitments—which is what all the so called "welching" was really about.

The MST would meet with members, take their requests, run them by Aspin, record commitments, follow-up with members in writing to ensure Aspin received credit for his actions, and "whip" important votes in the committee and on the House floor that were important to the Chairman. ("Whipping" stems from the British parliamentary system in which members are asked to support or oppose a certain measure, and the votes are counted in advance so that leadership can judge whether or not their position will prevail when the real vote takes place.)

This last part was controversial. Many members had grown accustomed to working their special requests for inclusion in the Defense Authorization bill through other staff members, bypassing the chairman altogether. And then some would vote against the overall bill, which allowed them at times to have their cake and eat it too (vote no against the overall measure on principle or partisan grounds, while still getting their special interest item over the finish line).

After MST was established, this practice stopped, at least for as long as Aspin was chairman. From then on, if a member of Congress asked for—and received—a provision in the annual defense bill, that member was expected to vote yes on the overall bill. If the member chose to vote no, he or she was welcome to do so, but their special interest item would likely get dropped in conference. This was the new rule, and MST's job was to enforce it.

Larry was on the hunt for certain types of people to round out the Member Services Team. As team leader, he would be the top interface with the most senior Members. He needed what he called "Doer A" to carry the load with the mid-level members and "Doer B" who could assist with the more junior members; both Doer A and Doer B needed to have the right blend of deference and moxy to successfully interact with members of Congress—showing enormous respect for their positons yet holding the line to ensure the rule about voting for the bill was followed.

Next was the "political computer," someone with great attention to detail who could devise a system to keep track and follow up on all commitments. The political computer also kept the "whip counts" on all important measures.

Because Aspin liked to build consensus for his policy positions and gain visibility for himself through organizing and participating in working dinners and seminars, the next position, "Pam II," was very important. Nicknamed for Pamela Harriman, a consummate Washington host and future US Ambassador to the UK, "Pam II" was charged with planning events over which Aspin would preside—these events actually became a "hot ticket" in Washington and helped Aspin build political consensus for his policy approaches.

The last member of MST was a jack-of-all-trades administrative assistant who helped with everything, including scheduling.

Within the new team, I became Doer A. I was able to "give" the team institutional memory of the committee processes, staffers, and some members of Congress based on my eight years of tenure. What I "got" from MST was experience in the world of political operations, issue exposure beyond personnel and compensation, and a broader network within the halls of Congress. Although each member of the team had a different background and skill set, each could tell a similar story about giving and getting.

From the earliest days our team formed, we knew what the vision and goals were. Each of us believed in a strong defense and in the Aspin approach on the most important issues of the day. Each of us knew that important work could only be achieved in Congress if you could successfully blend the right policy with the right politics. And each of us was committed and loyal to the Chairmanship of Les Aspin.

We approached each member discussion, each vote, and each policy event with drive and energy. And when the times got rough, as they did from time to time, we supported one another like family. We celebrated frequently when we prevailed; when there was failure, Larry, as team leader, accepted responsibility and then we collectively figured out how the team would do better next time.

Finally, we had passion for our work and for each other. Like I said, this was my family during hard times. I will never forget one occasion in which we were collecting amendments to be considered for adoption during the Committee debate on the annual defense authorization bill.

The rub was that there were deadlines associated with submitting these amendments, and if you missed the deadline, your amendment would be disqualified from consideration and debate.

This is precisely what happened in the case of one senior Democratic member and her amendment; her staffer missed the submission deadline but tried to bully me into accepting the amendment anyway. I held my ground and said no.

An argument ensued, and his and my voice both got louder. He then grabbed me by the shoulders, yelled about two inches from my face and pulled me down a short flight of steps. I almost went airborne and fell on top of him. What happened next was horrifying. While restraining me with one hand, he pulled back the other and made a fist. I was completely convinced at that moment that he was about to punch me in the face. Fortunately, another man appeared and grabbed his hand. The moment he let go of me, I proceeded to run—not walk—from the room without uttering a word. I made it back to my office before descending into sobs and shaking uncontrollably.

When Larry found out about this, he promised me that "this would not stand." Aspin was prepared to brush the whole thing off as a dispute among staff, but Larry insisted that a full investigation be conducted. Aspin ultimately agreed.

The next few months were incredibly awkward. Many looked at me oddly after this incident (I think many blamed me for not yielding), but I remember the MST team being a bulwark of support for me. When the investigation concluded, the man was fired outright for his actions. He tried to save his job by writing a letter of apology, but to no avail.

Bottom line—MST was a great team and we had all five hallmarks: 1) The give and get, 2) A clear vision, 3) Drive and energy,

4) Celebrations and accountability, and 5) passion for our work and each other.

Moreover, my boss and team backed me to the hilt throughout a dark experience—we were family. And more than twenty-five years later, we still are.

## TALENT DEPLOYMENT IS A FORCE MULTIPLIER

Through an extensive study on organizational time, talent, and energy, Bain & Company has found that, depending on your role, difference-making talent is two to twelve times better than an average performer in the same role in the same industry. Teams comprised of high-performing, "all-star" individuals with inspirational leaders thereby act as a force multiplier on productivity.

Better teams have team members that are able to contribute more to the final product, provide greater leverage, and build on the strengths of other team members. Great leaders are then able to add more value on top of this.

However, it is not enough to have star talent alone—talent deployment, or allocating the talent to the most business-critical tasks, drives the biggest difference in productive power. The best companies are 25 percent more productive due to the way they deploy difference-making talent.

(Top) *I briefed President Obama in the Oval Office about the changes we made within the nuclear enterprise. (Chapter 13)*

(Left) *Today, when I return to the Pentagon and visit "within the glass doors," there is a new portrait displayed side by side with the twenty-one men and one woman who preceded me as Secretary of the Air Force. (Chapter 18)*

Susie Hadid Photo

(Top) *When my daughter Regina married my son-in-law Colin, she asked me to walk her down the aisle. When I married Frank two years earlier, my son Sam gave me away. Here we are on Regina's wedding day: Frank (left), Sam (right), and Colin (second from right). (Chapter 7)*

(Bottom) *Briefing reporters in the Pentagon press room about the cheating scandal within the nuclear enterprise. Lieutenant General Seve Wilson, Commander of Global Strike Command, is at my side. (Chapter 13)*

(Top) *Visiting with airmen at Creech Air Force Base during the "Investigate" phase of the RPA (Drone) pilot review. Behind me is the Predator. (Chapter 16)*

(Bottom) *Wherever I traveled, I spoke regularly with airmen at "All Calls"—the military equivalent of Town Hall meetings—about the important issues facing the Air Force, including our efforts to combat sexual assault and "stop doing stuff." (Chapters 14 and 17)*

(Top) *Visiting Pueblo, Colorado with the first four enlisted RPA (Drone) pilot candidates. By 2020, one half of the Global Hawk pilot force will be enlisted.* (Chapter 16)

(Bottom) *Conducting a focus group session with members of the nuclear enterprise. I asked their leaders to leave the room in order to hear directly and candidly from frontline airmen.* (Chapter 13)

*One of the fun things about being Secretary of the Air Force was taking selfies with the airmen. (Chapter 15)*

*I led two Lean In Circles while serving as Secretary of the Air Force. Although these peer to peer mentoring groups frequently are female only, I wanted my circles to include both women and men. (Chapter 4)*

(Top and Bottom) *Presenting and defending the Air Force budget to Congress was one of my top jobs. I worked closely with members one-on-one (seen here with Senators Jeanne Shaheen [NH] and Bill Nelson [FL] of the Senate Armed Services Committee) and during Congressional hearings (testifying before the House Appropriations Subcommittee on Defense.) (Chapter 12)*

*Secretary of Defense Chuck Hagel selected me for the Secretary of the Air Force position. General Mark Welsh was the first Chief of Staff I worked with. Both were with me during my swearing in ceremony. (Chapter 12)*

*With Brian Williams at the Warrior Games in West Point, New York. After the Air Force seated volleyball team won the Gold medal, Brian gave his medal to me. I will always remember this special moment and be grateful for Brian's service. (Chapter 10)*

## PART 3

# GET THINGS DONE

# CHAPTER 12

# Becoming SECAF

N O MATTER WHAT PURPOSE YOU CHOOSE to pursue in life, accomplishing goals—getting things done—is what ultimately counts.

It's what separates the good professionals from the great professionals and will help you achieve the next level of leadership. Although getting a promotion in your chosen field is supposed to signal management's belief in your future potential (and that's typically true), make no mistake about it—management will also want to understand your body of accomplishment in your current and previous roles. That means Get Things Done!

As I said earlier, being chosen as SECAF was the honor of my professional life and gave me the opportunity to Get Things Done for more people and in a bigger way than I had ever experienced. I was anxious to get started. Let's go fast!

Ironically, the nomination and confirmation process took way longer than I thought or hoped. But on the positive side, it gave me more time to think through the goals I would establish once I became Secretary of the Air Force and how I would implement my five-step approach to Get Things Done: Investigate, Communicate, Activate, Iterate, and Follow-up. I'll tell you more about the five-step approach shortly.

First, let me tell you how the nomination and confirmation process unfolded for me.

After I was told of my selection for the job in March 2013, I had to fill out hundreds of pages of financial disclosures and reapply for a security clearance (I already had one, so this seemed particularly redundant). I then submitted all of my paperwork to the White House and the waiting game began.

The White House vetting took several months, during which time I married Frank and continued to work as Sector President at SAIC. By now, the company knew that I was about to be nominated and was in the process of selecting my successor. I was finally nominated on August 1, 2013, after which Congress promptly left town for a nearly one-month recess period.

Once nominated, I was able to begin receiving briefings from Pentagon officials to help me prepare for my confirmation hearing and paying "courtesy calls" to Senators who would eventually vote on my nomination. As context, under the Constitution, the President nominates, but the Senate advises and gives consent on the President's nominees, a power the Senate guards religiously.

The listening part of communication is the most useful skill when visiting Senators. More often than not, they raised parochial issues to me about a military base in their states, or a favored weapon system that was manufactured back home. To the extent broader issues were raised, the number one issue was sexual assault in the military and the belief that the Air Force was not sufficiently committed to taking the steps necessary to take care of victims, punish perpetrators, and change the culture.

The number two issue was the need to fund defense at higher levels. (Almost all of the Senators who asked to meet with me were defense hawks and believed we were underfunding our military.)

The number three issue was most disturbing of all—many Senators seemed angry with the Air Force. They complained that they were not always given sufficient heads up when there was either good news or bad news forthcoming, particularly news that affected their states. They also felt that the Air Force had flip-flopped on issues pertaining to budget and policy matters: the Air Force position would be one way this year and 180 degrees different the next year.

My job at this stage was not to rebut or defend, rather to take it all in, be non-committal on policy issues, and to promise follow-up if confirmed.

I prepared big time for my confirmation hearing before the Senate Armed Services Committee in September 2013. Luckily, I was on a panel with three other nominees. No question—there is safety in numbers. With four nominees, I was unlikely to receive more than a quarter of the questions.

My opening statement focused on the three priorities I intended to pursue as Secretary of the Air Force, if confirmed: 1) Take Care of People, 2) Strike the right balance between Readiness Today (training, etc.), and Modernization for Tomorrow (new technologies and weapons), and 3) Make Every Dollar Count (make the Air Force the most efficient organization possible).

Why did I pick these priorities?

A little bit of background is in order here.

Taking Care of People was very much in line with my overall philosophy about doubling down on people issues no matter what the organization or circumstance. Moreover, the Air Force I encountered in 2013 was quite a bit different than the one I remembered from the 1990s. In the first place, the Air Force had gotten a lot smaller over time—200,000 people smaller to be exact. After the fall of the Soviet Union in the early 1990s, military personnel numbers were reduced overall because the threat had fundamentally changed, though no one at that time predicted the advent of the war on terror. After September 11, 2001, the military was ordered into operations in Afghanistan and Iraq, which meant that a significantly smaller force had to work harder and harder—with more overseas deployments and less time at home for fundamental training and family time. I was aware that there were certain strains within the force but did not understand the degree of the problem at this point.

When it came to Readiness and Modernization, and striking the right balance between the two, the entire federal government in 2013 was in the throes of something called "sequestration"—a process agreed to by the President and the Congress. This was mainly because they were unable to agree on the specifics of how to reduce the country's debt and deficit (at the time, our debt was considered to be a huge national security threat). With no agreement on what to do, they set in motion a very regrettable, automatic process that reduced almost every account in the defense and non-defense parts of government by the same amount—shared pain, you might say—which inflicted a lot of damage on many important programs. The point here is that readiness and modernization (and people for that matter) requires money, and money was in relatively short supply. Tradeoffs would need to be made because the budget could not accommodate every request.

This led me to Make Every Dollar Count. I recognized that we owed it to the taxpayers to look for dollar savings, ways to avoid costs, and to free up the time of an already too-busy force. I am grateful to General Larry Spencer, the first Vice Chief of Staff I served with, for allowing me to steal this slogan. Larry launched the initial Make Every Dollar Count campaign, which involved taking suggestions from airmen in the field about ways to save money. Ultimately, I expanded the campaign to include other cost-saving and time-saving initiatives. You'll read more about one of these initiatives—"Stop Doing Stuff"—in Chapter 17.

Overall, the hearing went well, and I hoped for a speedy confirmation; unfortunately, it was not to be. A single Senator immediately put me "on hold"—a privilege permitted under Senate rules. This Senator had no problem with my qualifications or me; she believed that a favorite weapon system might be cut in the following year's budget, so she held me as hostage to extract large amounts of data from the Air Force. Until she lifted her hold, my nomination could not go forward.

Within a few weeks, more than a thousand pages of information were presented to the Senator and she lifted her hold. But within hours, another Senator put me on hold for a different reason.

One of the longest holds came from a group of bipartisan Senators representing the "ICBM Caucus." This group was concerned that as the DOD marched toward meeting the New START Treaty nuclear reduction mandates, one of their states would sustain a base closure. They held my nomination from moving forward in an effort to obtain reassurances from the Pentagon that no base closure would occur.

And so it went for months.

Finally, the logjam broke free for me five months after I was nominated, and my name was put to a vote. I was confirmed on December 13, 2013 by a vote of 79-6.

Now the most challenging part began: Get Things Done.

My approach to achieving goals and problem solving has five parts:

1. **Investigate**

   This means gather facts, seek views from multiple perspectives, and review alternative courses of actions.
   Depending on the issue, the investigate phase can be
   lengthy or extremely short. It all depends on the urgency
   and complexity of the challenge. And get used to ambiguity—no matter how much fact-finding you perform, you
   will never obtain all the facts.

2. **Communicate**

   Make the case for action and build buy-in from key
   members of the team. Then communicate to the broader
   audience. It's okay to use written communications (like a
   memo or email), but don't rely on the written word alone.
   It's very important to invest personal time and attention to
   communicating verbally—and don't be afraid to repeat the
   message frequently until it sinks in and resonates.

3. **Activate**

   Decide on the specific courses of action to pursue and
   launch! Start small and scale if necessary. Focus on what
   you can control, look for some quick wins, and then communicate those wins to the team. Finally, double down on
   people issues. Like I said before, if you can get the people
   part right, the other pieces are more likely to fall into place.

4. **Iterate**

   You probably won't get everything right, especially not in
   the beginning, so be prepared to shift gears if an initiative is
   not producing the results you expected. Jettison some ideas
   completely and be on the hunt for new ones to add. Also,
   be prepared to compromise and negotiate with others on

implementation and keep communicating-both successes and failures. This shows authenticity in leadership.

5. **Follow Up**

Once and done has never worked for me. I find that relentless follow-up is essential to ensure that something new remains on track. You need to stick with it because new approaches are often met with disbelief or pushback. Keep your cool with the team you are depending on to help implement but remain firm in the direction. Be prepared to devote significant amounts of personal time to the follow-up if it's important to you—and measure everything possible. When the team realizes that you will not give up and that you expect periodic progress updates with data, they will understand that this is, indeed, a top priority.

I will now tell you five stories—you might call them case studies—that illustrate how this five-part process helped me Get Things Done as Secretary of the Air Force.

# CHAPTER 13

# Case Study 1:
# The Nuclear Enterprise

AFTER THREE WEEKS OF SETTLING into the job, I was feeling pretty confident about where we were going. I had worked hard to establish a good professional relationship with the Chief of Staff of the Air Force, General Mark Welsh. It is extremely important for a political appointee like me to have a close working relationship with the senior uniformed military leaders. Although the United States has long operated under the principle of civilian control of the military, whenever a civilian leader directly butts heads with a military leader, the civilian frequently loses.

I also had the beginnings of my team surrounding me. I felt especially blessed that Eric Fanning was the Undersecretary of the Air Force (the number two civilian position) and had been the Acting Secretary for about six months prior to my confirmation. Eric and I had a long history together, dating back more than twenty years when we were both on the staff of the House Armed Services Committee—Eric was "Doer B" on the Member Services Team—and subsequently worked with me at Business Executives for National Security. Eric would go on to eventually be the Secretary of the Army—the first openly gay individual to hold such a post.

Finally, with the help of my front office team (consisting of various military assistants, an aide, and an administrative assistant), I had laid out a six-month master plan of activities and travel designed to highlight major budget and policy themes that needed attention. I was focused on my three priorities: people issues (including the need to keep fighting sexual assault and harassment), balancing readiness and modernization issues, and initiatives to make the Air Force more efficient.

So far, so good.

But then that email about cheating within the nuclear enterprise arrived.

Remember I told you about this in the Introduction?

Here came the first big zig-zag.

My military assistant, Colonel Steve Oliver, was the first to bring it to my attention. He assured me that there are many checks and balances in the nuclear enterprise and that a cheating and drug investigation did not equate to a lack of safety.

I wasn't buying it.

I called General Welsh to make sure he had seen the news. He had, and we quickly agreed that we needed more information— and fast. So we assembled the key people, who briefed more details about both the checks and balances of the nuclear enterprise, as well as the state of play on the investigation at that point. Over the course of the next two days, we deliberated about possible courses of action and immediate next steps. I became increasingly comfortable that, although this incident represented a major failure of integrity on the part of some, the checks and balances within the system were strong and the weapons were, indeed, safe and secure.

The team also reminded me during these crash course sessions about the recent history of the nuclear enterprise—something I only vaguely remembered. Indeed, this cheating scandal was not the first incident in recent years that called into question the readiness of our nuclear forces.

Most notably, back in 2007, cruise missiles loaded with nuclear warheads were mistakenly loaded onto a B52H bomber and flown from Minot Air Force Base, North Dakota, to Barksdale Air Force Base, Louisiana. The missiles with the nuclear warheads were not reported missing and remained mounted to the aircraft at both Minot and Barksdale for about thirty-six hours, during which time they were not properly protected. In another incident, a shipment of non-nuclear critical components (incorrectly labeled) was sent from FE Warren Air Force Base in Wyoming and the shipment ended up in Taiwan. These two occurrences, along with several reports and investigations, triggered then Secretary of Defense Bob Gates to fire both the Secretary of the Air Force and the Chief of Staff of that era. All of this, plus drunk and disorderly behavior by a major nuclear commander in, of all places, Russia, and his subsequent firing received extensive press coverage and caused some to question whether there was "rot" within the nuclear forces.

By the way, after each previous scandal, task forces were formed, and investigations were conducted. No fewer than twenty reports about the nuclear enterprise were drafted during the period 2007 through late 2013 with more than 1,500 separate recommendations about how to improve it. Most of the recommendations were implemented. Yet here we were again with a new set of problems that called into question the safety and security of these formidable weapons.

After the first set of briefings, I directed that the entire unit at Malmstrom Air Force Base in Montana retake the test in question within the next few days. First, we needed to assure ourselves that the missileers standing watch, in fact, were competent to perform the mission. We also reported the occurrence to the Secretary of Defense and to the Chairman of the Joint Chiefs of Staff, who were charged with informing the President about key nuclear matters.

We then discussed a public affairs strategy—what, if anything, should we tell Congress and the American people about the incident?

Some argued that we do nothing, as the initial report came via the classified network, and this wasn't that big of a deal anyway. We would make a bigger deal out of it than it merited if we commented. Others talked about how bad news like this would surely leak, so we needed to be ready with a "response to query"—just in case. Notably, Brigadier General Les Kodlick, the Chief of Air Force Public Affairs, was the outlier in the discussion. He argued that General Welsh and I should go on the offense: that this matter was so important, we should call a special press conference to announce the news ourselves.

My instincts were identical to those of BG Kodlick.

Just as I had learned in the City Time Scandal, bad news just gets worse with time, and a response to query after a leak allows others (not you) to shape the story and put you on the defense.

So preparations were hastily made to conduct a press conference the following day—it would be the first time I appeared before the Washington press corps as Secretary of the Air Force. I remembered what the Senators told me when I made my office calls (namely that they frequently felt blindsided by the Air Force), so before we went public with the bad news, I personally called members of the Montana Congressional delegation to tell them what was about to hit.

The press conference was scheduled for 2:30 p.m. on Thursday, January 16, 2014. The team had prepared an opening statement for me, which I remember totally rewriting with only minutes to go. I wanted to be as forceful, plain-spoken, and authentic as possible, and the words needed to reflect my own voice.

When the time came, I stepped up to the podium with the Chief of Staff, General Welsh, at my side. I told the press what we knew, what we did not yet know, how we intended to find out, and reassured everyone that problems would get fixed and that people would be held accountable. By now, I was able to report that we had retested almost all missileers and that the vast majority passed the proficiency test with flying colors. I committed to provide periodic updates as we learned more from our investigation and made any changes. Above all else, I delivered the message: the nuclear enterprise was safe and secure.

General Welsh and I then took questions from reporters and exited the press room. I let out a big sigh of relief. That went about as well as could be expected, though the ensuing press coverage was all negative (just one more thing wrong with the nuclear enterprise).

The real pressure was only just beginning. And, for me, the bottom line was: in the midst of many conflicting opinions in Washington, I could either continue to listen and debate, or I could Get Things Done.

Walking back to my office, I turned to Colonel Steve Oliver, my military assistant. "Remember that six-month travel plan we created?" I asked.

"Yes Ma'am," he replied. "We're on track to depart for San Antonio, Texas, to visit our Basic Training facility as our first stop."

"Rip up the program," I said. "There's been a change of plans. I want to visit our ICBM bases to see for myself what's going on. And I want to leave Monday."

For context, there are five US Air Force nuclear bases within the United States that are home to the land based intercontinental ballistic missiles (ICBMs), nuclear capable bombers, or both. Three of them—all of which have ICBMS—are located in Northern tier states: Wyoming, Montana, and North Dakota. A fourth, which hosts bombers only as well as the Global Strike Command (the oversight command of all things nuclear in the Air Force), is in Louisiana. I visited all four of these bases in a four-day period. (I eventually visited the fifth as well, but not on this trip.) General Welsh also visited the four bases, but he did so on a different schedule. I was accompanied by Major General Jack Weinstein, the two-star commander of 20th Air Force, which is the oversight command of all ICBM forces.

For those of you who are not familiar with military and military planning, suffice it to say that it was a big deal for a Secretary of the Air Force to announce suddenly, late on a Thursday, that she would be arriving at a base the following Monday. This sort of thing just wasn't done. Such a short time frame did not allow for the type of preparation that local commanders usually like to devote to a base visit. Moreover, there was a different format I wanted to follow: Yes, I wanted to receive briefings about mission, conduct leadership discussions with commanders, and tour facilities.

That was pretty standard.

But I also wanted to do focus group discussions with groups of front-line airmen—different job specialties and different ranks—and I did not want the leaders present for these discussions.

Not standard at all.

My reasoning was that, in addition to hearing the senior leaders' opinions, I also wanted input from lower-level individuals—and I reasoned I might get them to be more open with me if their bosses weren't present.

To say that this weeks' worth of visits was eye-opening would be a gross understatement. The focus groups with airmen were particularly enlightening. Although a lot of attention was devoted to the missileers, there were other key participants in the mission with whom I also spoke: security forces personnel who guarded the weapons and surrounding area, maintenance personnel who kept aged equipment operational, even facilities managers and chefs who provided food and lodging for those who deployed out to the remote sites for their long shifts.

And what I heard was not encouraging—overall, the airmen felt that leaders in Washington were talking out of both sides of their mouth—although everyone spoke about how important the nuclear enterprise was, we didn't put our money and attention where our mouth was. The equipment was old, facilities were sagging, and many had quality-of-life complaints. Some of the missileers who'd graduated from the prestigious Air Force Academy even told me that they cried, or their friends offered condolences, when it was revealed senior year that they would be assigned to the missile force. That's how unpopular and unappreciated the field had become.

Many of the support personnel complained about getting "stuck" in the Northern Tier bases (cold weather and mostly rural areas) and having been tainted with the "nuclear stink." And many spoke about a culture of extreme micromanagement, where even the slightest deviation from standard became a big failure. And here was a key insight: the speculation among missileers not involved with the cheating incident was that their colleagues had not cheated to pass; rather, they had cheated to get a perfect 100 percent score. This was because commanders were using perfect scores to differentiate between who would get promoted and who would not.

Talk about putting in place the wrong incentives for training and testing.

The other eye-opening experience was visiting a launch control center, which we did at FE Warren Air Force Base in Wyoming. Launch control centers are the deep underground bunkers where two missileers at a time pull twenty-four-hour shifts or alerts. These facilities typically are located hours from the actual base, so the airmen who deploy out there must build significant travel time into the already lengthy schedule. Road conditions are treacherous in the winter, and the temperature is bone-chilling cold.

We rode out to what seemed the middle of nowhere and came upon a fenced-in area with several non-descript brown buildings. Armed security personnel met us at the gate, checked credentials, and permitted entry. The above-ground facility is fairly basic—call it the living quarters for some of the support personnel. There is a kitchen, bathroom, communal bedroom with bunk beds, and a living room with a pool table, TV, games, and some books. All the furniture, flooring, and equipment sagged with age.

To go below, there is more security to pass through as well as massively-thick concrete doors. Then onto an elevator that travels slowly (very slowly) seven stories underground. The door opens and we, once again, came across another massive door and then into the launch capsule. This small space is where the missileers actually work and take turns sleeping in a cot behind a green curtain.

While working, the missileer is looking at a control panel with screens, green blips, and dials that look like something out of the 1950s or 1960s. Indeed, in most cases, this equipment and the facilities date back to that era. The green blips are actually incoming messages from various sources, designed to constantly test whether or not the airmen are properly conducting alert or focused on maintenance issues (maintenance is a very big deal when you are talking about weapons as old as the ICBM force). The messages arrive in the form of scrambled letters, which then must be decoded and verified using nearby classified binders.

In the event of a real incident (like the President communicating a command to launch a nuclear weapon), it would take *both* missileers, plus two others in a separate underground facility, to verify the order. Then all four would need to open locked containers, obtain special keys, and insert the keys into the controls (Turns out there are no "nuclear buttons" in the White House or in launch control facilities.)

Bottom Line: The United States maintains 24/7/365 nuclear launch capabilities—and our potential adversaries around the world know it. This is what deterrence is all about, and it has kept us free of a World War III environment for seventy years. So even though these weapons have never been fired other than for testing and training, the airmen who are responsible for them are fulfilling a vital mission to protect the homeland each and every day.

But that's not the way it felt to most of them. Their morale was very low.

Returning to Washington, I compared notes with General Welsh and with Lt. General Seve Wilson, the Commander of Global Strike Command. All of us were coalescing around an initial set of observations. We had the opportunity to brief Secretary Hagel (who by now had ordered his own joint review, involving the Navy nuclear enterprise as well). And I believed we needed to update Congress and the press, all of whom were clamoring for more information and impressions.

The week of January 27, 2014 was a big one. We set up several briefings on Capitol Hill, mostly for Congressional staff from the Armed Services Committees and the ICBM Caucus.

I also conducted my second press conference, this time with General Wilson at my side, providing an update on the cheating investigation. I then launched into the BLUF from my base visits— what I called my "Seven Key Observations."

1. The problems with the nuclear forces were more extensive than an isolated cheating incident. There were systemic issues that needed to be addressed. Specifically, the culture was one of micromanagement, fear that small infractions would be career-enders, and a zero-defect mentality existed even when training. Morale was suffering. (Though it did not seem this way at the time, this observation about culture was the most startling to many because it was the first time an official government representative admitted on the record that there were systemic factors at play.)

2. We needed to have accountability for the cheating incident—for both leaders and airmen. I promised this would be the case.

3. Somewhere along the line, we had lost the distinction between training and testing. I said I did not believe the missileers cheated to pass the test; they likely cheated to get a 100 percent test score because this was the route to promotion. We needed to move away from a culture of constant testing and preparing to test and toward a culture of training and continuous improvement.

4. Even though leaders had spoken of the nuclear mission for years as being number one, that's not the way our people felt, nor did our budget and policy choices reflect that. Specifically, I said I thought we needed to make the career field more attractive to young people joining the Air Force and needed to provide better professional development for our nuclear airmen.

5. Our nuclear enterprise/nuclear career field needed more incentives and accolades if we wanted to attract the best going forward.

6. We needed to invest in the readiness of the current generation of weapons and start to modernize for the next generation. In other words, we needed to put our money where our mouth was.

7. We needed to recommit across the entire Air Force to our core values: Integrity First, Service Before Self, and Excellence In All We Do. After all, what happened at Malmstrom was a failure of integrity.

So far in the story, I have been pursuing the Investigate and Communicate part of the Problem-Solving Approach. Now, the time had come to Activate.

I ordered two immediate actions. The first was called a Commander Directed Investigation of the actual cheating incident. This review, led by a General officer outside the nuclear enterprise, supplemented the law enforcement action already in process and ultimately led to appropriate accountability measures. The second was called the Force Improvement Program (FIP), under the day-to-day direction of Lt. General Wilson.

Over the course of the next few months, the FIP was all about getting input from Airmen on how to improve the nuclear mission. It was a series of focus groups, much like the ones I had done at each nuclear base. By listening primarily to those on the front lines, we developed a plan for improving all aspects of how the nuclear mission was accomplished—from training to work environments.

Here are some of the actions that came out of the FIP, the Commander Directed Investigation and our other efforts:

▶ We made the environment less micromanaged by pushing decision making on many areas down to a lower level. In other words, we made an effort to empower our people;

▶ We revamped the culture of constant testing to one of continuous improvement. Needless to say, no longer were 100 percent test scores used to promote—or not promote—our airmen;

▶ We elevated the three-star Global Strike Command to a four-star position and the senior nuclear advisor on the Air Staff from a two-star to a three-star position. Rank counts big time in the military so having higher ranking officers representing the nuclear enterprise at the key decision-making tables should go a long way to help advocate for policy and resources in the future;

▶ On accountability, seven commanders at Malmstrom lost their jobs, and the missileers involved with cheating were punished according to their degree of involvement;

▶ We pumped significant additional resources into the upkeep of existing facilities and equipment, launched modernization programs to produce the next generation of ballistic missiles and bomber forces, and addressed personnel shortages in key career specialties;

▶ In terms of making the career field more exciting to young people and upping the ante on professional development:

▶ We offered scholarships and bonuses;

▶ We added accolades, like the Nuclear Deterrence Operations Service Medal; and

▶ We boosted professional development opportunities.

▶ Finally, we launched a number of efforts across the entire Air Force to rededicate ourselves to the Air Force Core Values: Integrity, Service Before Self, and Excellence in All We Do.

Like I said earlier, the Iterate and Follow Up parts of problem solving are important. Once and done never cuts it.

On Iterate, we changed the population of bonus recipients twice before we became comfortable that all who were deserving had been included. And when it came to Follow Up, I held regular meetings to review progress and visited the nuclear bases four additional times during my three-year tenure. On each occasion, I not only visited with leaders, I also visited privately with airmen so that I could assess whether or not they were actually feeling the changes we had instituted from Washington. And I spoke about the nuclear enterprise frequently in all public remarks. Words and actions finally were beginning to come together.

The nuclear enterprise was the driving reason behind my first meeting with President Obama in August 2014. (Recall that I was selected for the Air Force job by Secretary Hagel and had never actually met the President. With the nuclear scandal all over the news, though, the President was asking questions.) Secretary Hagel and then Chairman of the Joint Chiefs, Martin Dempsey, regularly provided updates to the President, but in August of 2014, I had the opportunity to accompany them to the Oval office and do the talking on nuclear matters.

Vice President Biden also was present (I previously met him in June of 2014 when he was the commencement speaker at the Air Force Academy—a speaking honor I would have in 2016) as were the National Security Advisor, Susan Rice, and her Deputy, Tony Blinken.

It's a heady experience to brief the President and Vice President in the Oval Office about a weighty national security issue. It's a good thing that I have a picture of the occasion—I was so nervous, I forgot to breathe in the décor of my surroundings.

After introductions were made, I launched into a twenty-minute update of all the changes made within the nuclear enterprise since the cheating scandal hit. The President and Vice President were very engaged and asked questions about people and training issues. When I got to the part about providing more professional development for the airmen in the nuclear job specialties, both men asked for more details.

Many people—including some within the Air Force—considered President Obama to be anti-nuclear. In fact, when I traveled to the nuclear bases and met with missileers, some of them cited President Obama's 2009 Prague speech in which he stated "America's commitment to seek the peace and security of a world without nuclear weapons" as evidence that he was against the nuclear mission, and by extension, they reasoned, against them. This was simply not true. President Obama and his White House team were extremely supportive of the people of the nuclear enterprise and of all military personnel, for that matter. Moreover, he ultimately approved moving forward with the development of the next generation of nuclear weapons, so he recognized that modernization of the arsenal was essential for maintaining the deterrent value of the triad. In addition, modernization was an important promise made to Congress in exchange for votes to pass the nuclear arms reduction treaty, New START.

Some forget that the President went on to say in Prague: "I'm not naïve. This goal (a world without nuclear weapons) will not be reached quickly—perhaps not in my lifetime. It will take patience and persistence. But now, we too, must ignore the voices of those who tell us that the world cannot change. We have to insist, Yes we can."

Although I was not a direct report to the President, I went on to see him on other occasions, both when the White House celebrated our military personnel and families or for meetings related to space (the Air Force is responsible for most of the national security satellites in orbit).

However, I never again briefed him on the issues related to the nuclear enterprise, because the situation was now on a good path.

And I was reminded yet again of how a lot of good can come from something bad, provided that you <u>Investigate</u>, <u>Communicate</u>, <u>Activate</u>, <u>Iterate</u>, and <u>Follow-Up</u>.

## THE IMPORTANCE OF PSYCHOLOGICAL SAFETY WITHIN TEAMS

The nuclear enterprise has a "no fail" mission in the real world, but like all teams, when it comes to the training environment, personnel should feel safe to make mistakes, learn, and grow.

In the private sector, research from Google's People Operations identified key dynamics that set successful teams apart from other teams at Google, and the most important of those dynamics was psychological safety—the ability to feel safe to take risks and be vulnerable in front of your teammates. Paul Santagata, Head of Industry at Google identified strategies to increase psychological safety on his teams based on these findings.

His steps were:

1. Approach conflict as a collaborator, not an adversary. Think through "How could we achieve a mutually desirable outcome?"

2. Speak human to human. Remember that respect, competence, social status, and autonomy are universal needs.

3. Anticipate reactions and plan countermoves. Thinking through this in advance helps ensure your content is heard versus coming across as an attack.

4. Replace blame with curiosity. Using neutral, factual language and asking for solutions avoids defensiveness and disengagement.

5. Ask for feedback on delivery. Ask how you delivered your message, what worked, how it felt to hear the message, and how it could have been more effective.

6. Measure psychological safety. Google has survey questions to measure this, including "How confident are you that you won't receive retaliation or criticism if you admit an error or make a mistake?"

# CHAPTER 14

# Case Study 2:
# Fighting Sexual Assault
# and Harassment

IN 2013, THERE WAS NO MORE CONTROVERSIAL PERSONNEL CASE
than that of Lt. Colonel James Wilkerson and Lt. General Craig
Franklin. At the time, Lt. Colonel Wilkerson, an F16 pilot, was
serving as the Inspector General at Aviano Air Base in Italy; Lt.
General Franklin was the three-star senior military boss over most
US Air Force personnel in Europe.

In 2012, Wilkerson was found guilty in a military court of
aggravated sexual assault, abusive sexual contact, and three counts
of conduct unbecoming an officer for an incident in which he
allegedly assaulted a sleeping female houseguest. Wilkerson's wife
and nine-year-old son were present in the home at the time of
the assault, which occurred after a party at the Wilkerson house
concluded. According to the prosecution, the assault stopped only
because Mrs. Wilkerson entered the bedroom and saw her husband

in bed with the other woman. According to Mrs. Wilkerson, the event was a total fabrication; Lt. Colonel Wilkerson maintained his innocence throughout and did not testify at trial.

Under the Uniform Code of Military Justice (UCMJ)—a separate set of laws that govern military personnel—Wilkerson was permitted to appeal his conviction directly to the senior officer in charge of his command. That officer, Lt. General Craig Franklin, was the "convening authority" and as such had "absolute power to disapprove the findings and sentence, or any part thereof, for any or no reason, legal or otherwise."

At trial, it came down to which version of events the jurors believed and who seemed more credible.

No question, Wilkerson was on the losing side of credibility with the jury, not only evidenced by his conviction but also by his sentence—one year in prison and dismissal from the military, including forfeiture of all pay and benefits.

But General Franklin saw it differently. Although he was not present at trial, did not hear testimony from witnesses, and was not privy to juror deliberations, he did have access to the relevant files and transcripts—as well as the Wilkersons' direct appeal to him. General Franklin overturned the conviction, a decision that could not be challenged by anyone, not even the Secretary of Defense. Though he was not required to do so, General Franklin explained his decision in a six-page memo. Basically, he questioned the credibility of the accuser and expressed disbelief that a loving husband, doting father, and accomplished fighter pilot (who had been recommended for promotion) could have committed such an egregious act. Frequently called the "good soldier defense," those who knew Wilkerson one way simply could not fathom that he might behave very differently under different circumstances.

Congress exploded in the aftermath of the Franklin ruling. The Air Force and other military services were already under intense scrutiny for the perceived failure to take sexual assault and harassment seriously, and the Franklin ruling became the poster child of absolute power run amok. Secretary Hagel proposed changing the UCMJ to prevent this type of case from ever happening again and Congress conducted angry hearings with the all-male military chiefs called on the carpet as witnesses.

Previous sexual assault scandals through the decades—from the Navy's Tailhook in the early 1990s (in which more than a hundred drunken Navy and Marine Corps officers groped and assaulted both men and women at a professional symposium), to the 2009 Air Force Basic Training Scandal (in which more than forty female trainees were victimized sexually on some level by their instructors) were rehashed as proof points that sexual assault problems in the military were never fully addressed.

Adding insult to injury, it was subsequently discovered that Lt. Colonel Wilkerson had committed adultery and fathered a child out of wedlock several years earlier—the mother of the child came forward to tell her story after seeing the publicity on the assault case. "I guess it's grating on me that he has no accountability," she later told *Stars and Stripes*. She also said that Mrs. Wilkerson was aware of the affair and the child. Wilkerson relinquished all parental rights to the baby and probably hoped that no one would ever find out.

So much for the "good soldier," loving husband, and doting father defense. Because the statute of limitations had run out on the adultery charge and because there was no way to take back General Franklin's leniency in the assault case, Wilkerson was dealt with administratively and ultimately forced into retirement at the rank of Major—one rank below Lt. Colonel—the best punishment that could be achieved under the circumstances.

This was the atmosphere within the Air Force when I took office in 2013. And General Franklin was still in command in Europe.

I began discussing personnel issues with General Welsh almost from the beginning. The Secretary of the Air Force plays a major role in personnel selections at the three-star and four-star level, as well as with the assignments of the general officers at this level. It's important that senior military and civilian officials have the confidence of the Secretary. General Franklin was top of mind with me—and my confidence in him was in short supply.

As it turned out, he made the headlines once again with the case of a young airman accused of sexual assault. As General Franklin and his team debated how to proceed with the case, he declined to talk with the attorney who was assisting the victim (called the Special Victims' Counsel). He subsequently decided not to send the case to court martial. In other words, he made an important ruling in a second sexual assault case without first agreeing to hear the voice of the victim. How could a commander be so insensitive as to not be willing to listen to the victim, especially when the Air Force was under such pressure "to get serious" about sexual assault?

Bottom line: I did not think General Franklin was the right leader with the right judgment to continue commanding airmen in Europe—and I told General Welsh so. General Welsh pointed out that there was no other position for Franklin: that if he departed the job in Europe he would need to retire. But because he had not served three years as a three-star, he would, by law, have to retire as a two-star.

Unless I was willing to recommend a waiver. Would I do so? I said, "No way."

General Welsh was not happy with my decision on this, but I felt strongly that we needed to move on. He spoke to General Franklin shortly after Christmas in 2013. General Franklin announced his decision to retire shortly thereafter.

I spoke with General Franklin, at his request, via videoconference from Europe shortly before the news broke. I did not expect to like him, but I did. He came across as caring and sincere. He emphasized how much time he put into reviewing the Wilkerson case and clearly felt that he had been painted unfairly as "a good old boy protecting his fighter pilot friend." He became choked up when talking about his thirty-seven-year career and what an honor it had been to lead young airmen.

I thanked General Franklin for his decision to retire. With his departure, the Air Force could begin to put this chapter behind us. Little did I know...

WHEN SEXUAL ASSAULT HAPPENS—to a woman or to a man in the military—the victim has several recourses:

1. Keep your mouth shut and do nothing. Regrettably, our anonymous survey data suggests that this is what the majority of victims do, as they fear—and with good reason—possible retaliation and victim blaming if they pursue justice through the system.

2. The victim can seek a full investigation and ultimately justice by making an "unrestricted report." This is where the law enforcement arm of the Air Force—the Office of Special Investigation or OSI—will interview witnesses, gather evidence, and build a case file that could be used for trial or other forms of punishment. Additionally, the victim can

obtain legal counsel, medical care, and counseling, as well as the possibility of a reassignment away from the environment of the assault.

3. Report the matter in a confidential way (called a "restricted report" in military parlance). There are only a handful of officials who are allowed to accept restricted reports (all others must mandatorily report such matters to the appropriate authorities). Once a restricted report is filed, the victim can obtain legal counsel, medical care, and counseling (just as he or she may obtain if an unrestricted report is made) but cannot obtain a reassignment, and no investigatory follow up will occur. Very importantly, in the event the victim wants to remain confidential but accidentally reports to an official not permitted to accept a restricted report, he or she will lose control of the matter, and it will be subject to mandatory investigation.

After the Franklin matter was put to rest and I had completed my tour of the nuclear enterprise, I made an effort to return to the original six-month travel plan. As mentioned earlier, a visit to the Air Force Basic Training Base at Lackland near San Antonio, Texas, was at the top of my list. All young enlisted airmen (about thirty-five thousand each year), many of whom are eighteen to nineteen years old, spend eight weeks at the beginning of their Air Force tours at Lackland. At Lackland, the new airmen learn the essentials of military life: discipline; physical fitness; combat related skills; first aid; "buddy care" and chemical/biological weapons defense.

The Lackland experience is fundamental to how all new enlisted personnel begin life in the Air Force.

Yet Lackland is also the site of that major sexual assault scandal that began in 2009, involving more than forty female trainees who were victimized by their training instructors.

Shortly after traveling to Lackland, I visited the United States Air Force Academy in Colorado Springs, Colorado. The Academy is among the top universities in the country and the most prestigious avenue to becoming an Air Force officer (the other avenues are ROTC and Officer Candidate School). Set on more than eighteen thousand acres in the shadows of the rampart range of the Rocky Mountains, the Academy boasts extensive facilities for housing, academics, athletics, and research. One of the landmarks, known as the "Honor Wall" reminds cadets and visitors alike of the Cadet Honor Code: "We will not lie, cheat, or steal, nor tolerate among us anyone who does."

Without question, the Air Force Academy experience is fundamental to how many new officers begin life in the Air Force.

Yet the Academy is also the site of a major sexual assault scandal that first broke in 2003. Ultimately, it was uncovered that 12 percent of the women who graduated from the Academy in 2003 reported that while at the Academy, they were victims of rape, attempted rape, or another "penetrative or contact sexual assault." Seventy percent of those surveyed said they had experienced sexual harassment, of which 22 percent reported being pressured for sexual favors. Perhaps most damning of all, the belief was pervasive that leadership knew—or should have known—about these unacceptable behaviors but did little or nothing to stop them.

I could continue to recount stories about sexual assault and harassment (which affects men as well as women), but I think you get the picture. It was occurring in the Air Force, and most victims did not feel sufficiently supported—or supported at all.

As a woman who navigated through difficult, heavily male environments where dignity and respect were sometimes absent, I was determined to make a dent in this problem, especially now that I was the top leader of the Air Force.

So once again, I set out to Get Things Done using the five-step process. Over time, my team and I built a plan specifically targeted at combatting sexual assault.

My early visits to military bases, research about past incidents, and review of statistics and cases formed the backbone of my early efforts to Investigate military sexual assault and harassment. Just as I found it extremely helpful to talk to the front-line defenders within the nuclear enterprise, I also found it extremely helpful to talk to the front-line defenders of sexual assault victims. These individuals—known as Sexual Assault Response Coordinators, or SARCs—can be found at all military bases, including remote locations overseas.

Wherever I traveled, I would request private visits with the local SARC, plus volunteer "victim advocates" and "Special Victims' Counsel" if they were available. We would close the door and talk privately, without commanders being present, with the hope of having a frank conversation. Over time, I also talked to multiple sexual assault survivors—both women and men.

Summarizing what I heard from SARCs and other support staff in these private sessions:

▶ Most (particularly those who had been at this for years) felt their current commanders were committed to the fight;

▶ Past investigative practices were changing for the better (for example, there was a much greater willingness to believe the victim rather than blame the victim during the investigation); and

> ▶ Special Victims' Counsel were a godsend to victims (the
> Air Force was the first to assign legal counsel to victims; it
> became a best practice and was eventually replicated across
> the military).

From victims, I heard a less encouraging story. Depending on
when they entered the system and began to seek help or justice,
most victims felt less supported (from moderate support to poor
support). They tended to feel a high degree of "retaliation" frequently from others in the unit who had found out about the assault
and had taken the accused's side or from command action which
(either in fact or in perception) set them back in some way. Almost
all felt great disappointment with the military justice system.

On the question of the Uniform Code of Military Justice, over
the three years I held office, Congress directed many changes
to law that ultimately tied the hands of future commanders (I
believe in a good way). For example, the "good soldier" defense
was disallowed going forward, as was the ability of the convening
authority to overturn a court martial verdict. If the legal counsel to
a convening authority recommended a court martial, but the commander disagreed, the matter had to go to a higher-level authority
for resolution.

The only major proposal which did not go through was that
of Senator Kirsten Gillibrand and her supporters. She argued that
military commanders should be stripped of the decision to prose-
cute sexual assault and other serious crimes. Such authority should
be given to military prosecutors, according to the Senator.

The military was vehemently opposed to this idea. They argued
that retaining commanders (who were advised by legal counsel)
in the decision-making chain was crucial for "good order and discipline." Personally, I felt torn on the matter but ultimately sided

with the military as I could not see how simply shifting this decision point would produce more and better justice for victims. My preference was to keep commanders fully on the hook for what went on under their command.

Early on, I learned from the SARCs that the number of restricted and unrestricted reports is measured year over year. Through anonymous surveys, other data is also obtained—like how many military members experienced a sexual assault in a given year even if they did not report it. The anonymous survey also measured perceptions about retaliation—be it official from the chain of command or informal from friends and unit members who took sides. There also were separate statistics on the number of formal complaints made about harassment and retaliation. (Much like assault itself, harassment and retaliation are grossly underreported.)

Boiling this down to the essential, reports should go up (this means more people have greater confidence in the system and are willing to come forward) while actual incidents of assault and retaliation should go down year over year. And the number of formal complaints on harassment and retaliation should go up (which would, once again, show more confidence in the system).

Most SARCs believed (and this was borne out through the macro-level statistics) that confidence was growing across the board in all areas except retaliation. Good news, but there was still a long way to go.

The keeper of all this data for the Air Force—which eventually was compiled with other service data and reported to the Secretary of Defense and to Congress—was a two-star Air Force General known as the Director, Sexual Assault Prevention and Response Office. This official also was charged with staying on top of other related matters and helping the Chief of Staff and me figure out how to improve our approaches.

Those matters ranged from how we were taking care of victims (we weren't doing enough and we improved), to whether we should expand the pool of victim services to civilian employees (we did), to supporting victims during pretrial hearings (with Congress' help, we stopped the practice of defense counsel conducting lengthy public cross examinations of victims during pre-trial hearings), to what more should we do on prevention (we rolled out a five-year prevention strategy), to how to deliver the most effective training to the Force.

The Investigate, Communicate, Activate, and Iterate phases overlapped in a big way as I was learning more with each passing day. This was an area of some trial and error, as no one had or has a magic formula for ending sexual assault.

As I traveled, the Communicate phase was accomplished through "All-Calls" (town hall meetings) with troops at different locations. I made it a point at each stop to emphasize the importance of stopping sexual assault and harassment and how others need to stand in and stand up when they saw something headed in the wrong direction. This was an important part of my first priority—Taking Care of People. I told everyone that I was meeting with SARCs privately, demonstrating that I was putting personal time behind this priority and spoke out frequently about the need to stop sexual assault in other venues, like Congressional hearings and speeches.

The Activate part came over time as it became more apparent what was working and what was not. For example, we learned early on that lengthy presentations about sexual assault for all airmen once a year were not well received. Moreover, other than being able to say that the Air Force was training 100 percent of its people, the training probably was not having much impact. Many complained of "SARC fatigue" and sleeping through the presentations, which were often delivered in large auditoriums. It was clear we needed to Iterate.

So we did. The best training approach turned out to be shorter, bystander training where real sounding scenarios and (at times) actors would role-play situations and show how others could step in. By my final year in office, we decided to go with a form of interactive bystander training called "Green Dot," a program that teaches how to be an effective bystander, recognizing that everyone has barriers to their willingness to become involved. The motto of Green Dot is: "No one has to do everything, but everyone needs to do something."

The name Green Dot refers to a map used in training on which red dots indicate acts of violence. I went through the training myself, and I remember Dr. Dorothy Edwards, Green Dot's founder, likening the spread of red dots to a zombie apocalypse. A green dot is when someone intercedes in that act of violence before it gets out of control. The more green dots that appear, the less room there is for red dots. And that is the beginning of changing a culture.

There are three ways to intervene, known as the "3 Ds"—direct, deflect, and delegate. The direct option involves dealing directly with one or more of the people involved with the potentially violent situation. Deflect means doing something to diffuse the situation. Delegate means actively finding someone else to help.

Green Dot was the only program in existence at the time that had evidence of success in actually bringing down the rates of sexual assault and violence in high school communities. We decided to try it. It was central to the five-year Air Force-wide prevention strategy, which also called for hiring more than a hundred

new specialists across the force to build programs focused on preventing sexual assault in the first place.

The Follow Up phase on combatting Sexual Assault is crucial
and must never end. Frankly, if senior leaders drop the focus on
this one, I fear we may lose the momentum I hoped we achieved
during my tenure.

Earlier, I mentioned the two-star Director of the Air Force
Sexual Assault Prevention and Response office. A key part of my
Follow Up was to meet with this official monthly, to track prog-
ress on statistics, provide anonymous feedback I had received
from SARCs, and to stay abreast of how our initiatives were faring.
(During my tenure, I was honored to work with Major General
Gina Grosso and, subsequently, Major General James Johnson in
this capacity.)

One of my final acts as Secretary of the Air Force came in
December, 2016, when I reprimanded retired four-star general,
Arthur Lichte. This action came after a detailed investigation in
which it was found that the General had pressured a female subordinate into having sex with him. Had the statute of limitations
not passed, this case might have gone to court martial. But because
too much time had passed, the best option I had to show accountability was the reprimand and the initiation of a process called an
"officer grade determination"—this is when a separate military
board reviews conduct and helps assess the highest grade an individual served in uniform satisfactorily.

The bottom line to all of this: General Lichte was demoted from
a four-star general to a two-star, which cost him $50–75,000 per
year in retirement pay.

On February 1, 2017, a few weeks after I left office, the Air Force
released a redacted copy of the investigation, and reporter Tom
Vanden Brook wrote a front-page story about the case in *USA Today*.

Vanden Brook's article read in part:

*[General] Lichte drew a stinging letter of reprimand in December from Air Force Secretary Deborah James. James blasted Lichte for putting the officer 'in a position in which she could have believed that she had no choice but to engage in these sex acts, given your far superior grade, position and significant ability to affect her career'...*

Not all stories about misconduct reach the public domain. The fact that this story did is important.

It should send the message that no matter who you are and what your rank, if you engage in this type of behavior, your past will catch up with you.

## SEXUAL ASSAULT AND HARRASSMENT ARE PERVASIVE. HERE'S HOW TO HELP SURVIVORS:

Eighty-one percent of women and 43 percent of men have experienced some form of sexual harassment during their lifetime, and 38 percent of women have experienced sexual harassment at the workplace, according to a report done by a nonprofit, Stop Street Harassment. In addition to preventative and reactive actions an organization can take in response to sexual assault and harassment, there are also actions individuals can take to support survivors of sexual assault and harassment. The Joyful Heart Foundation, an organization that aims to help survivors heal, has several tips for how to support victims:

1. Listen actively. Respect and honor that talking about these topics takes courage.
2. Believe and validate. Survivors are often blamed for what happened to them and may feel ashamed and that they will not be believed.
3. Ask what you can do to help. Different individuals will need or want different things, and while you can make suggestions, defer to them for how you can help.
4. Offer resources. Many organizations specialize in helping survivors of sexual assault get the resources and support they need; you can help research options and resources.
5. Support them for as long as they need it. Check in periodically, as support often wanes in the days and weeks after the assault.
6. Know your limits. Be sure to replenish your own energy and manage your feelings so you can be a good friend to others and a good caretaker for yourself.

# CHAPTER 15

# Case Study 3:
# Making the Air Force
# More Diverse

WHILE THE FOCUS ON STOPPING SEXUAL ASSAULT was ongoing, I also wanted to pursue greater diversity and inclusion in the Air Force.

There are at least two important reasons why.

The first is the need to attract and retain the right kind of talent.

Like any employer, the armed forces seek out those who display intelligence, "stick-to-it-iveness," and important values. Unlike most other employers, the military also requires that individuals be within a certain age range, demonstrate strong physical fitness, and commit to accept multiple years of service and worldwide deployments.

Serving in the armed forces is special duty—and the military needs tens of thousands of qualified new individuals each year— which is why it needs to have the widest pool of people possible to draw from. And that pool in the US is increasingly diverse in race, gender, and ethnicity.

Here are a few telling statistics from a combination of the US Census Bureau and Pew Research data.

- ▶ In 2012, Latino, Asian, mixed race, and African-American births constituted the majority of births in the US for the first time in our history;

- ▶ By the 2044-2055 timeframe, non-Hispanic whites will cease to be the majority group in this country;

- ▶ 49 percent of babies born in the US are girls; and

- ▶ More than 50 percent of today's college graduates are women.

So if you think women and minorities are not important talent pools for the military to draw from, think again.

In addition to recruiting and retaining the best talent, the second reason to support more diversity and inclusion in the military relates to innovation. There are many studies in both the public and private sector that suggest that the best problem solving comes from diverse teams of people who collaborate together: people of different backgrounds, gender, races, ethnicities, education, and experience.

The old saying: "if all you have is a hammer, every problem begins to look like a nail" really applies.

So for these two reasons—talent and innovation—I stepped back early in my tenure as Secretary of the Air Force to Investigate just how we were doing on diversity in the Air Force.

The answer, I thought, was not good enough.

For example, the Air Force led the Department of Defense with the highest percentage of women in the force (nearly 20 percent)—that was pretty good though it fell far short of the potential for much higher numbers based on the female birth statistics. When it came to racial and ethnic diversity, on the other hand, we were in the middle of the pack for DOD.

Our junior enlisted force was quite diverse, but as rank went up, the percentage of females and minorities in the senior enlisted force went down. The same held true within the officer corps and among our civilians. Women, unfortunately, left the Air Force at twice the rate of men by the time they reached the mid-career point (eight to ten years of service). So we had a big retention problem.

For those of you who work in the private sector, does this issue sound familiar?

It should.

According to Department of Labor and Census Bureau data, women comprise about 47 percent of the labor force, and 59 percent of the college educated, entry-level workforce.

Yet, as you look at the higher ranks of corporate America, females comprise only 18 percent of S&P Board directors, 6 percent of CEOs, and 25 percent of executive level positions.

And here's one more diversity element to consider—this one relates to diversity of background and training. It may sound very specific to the Air Force, but I would submit that it translates extremely well to the private sector.

When it comes to the pilot career field (all manned pilot positions and most unmanned pilot positions—drones—are reserved for officers), minorities made up only 10 percent of the pilots, whereas they comprised 20 percent of the officer corps overall. Similarly, females made up 20 percent of the officer corps, but only 5 percent of pilots.

Stated another way, women and minorities were even more underrepresented in the pilot career field than they are in the overall Air Force.

The point about pilots and background is important. Although there are many career fields in the Air Force, at higher levels, pilots are deemed to be capable of serving in almost any capacity, whereas other career fields tend to get stove piped.

That is, fantastic cyber, nuclear, or space officers can aspire to serve in the upper echelons of the cyber, nuclear, or space fields, but at least so far, they have not had as many opportunities to lead in a broader capacity. Pilots, on the other hand, can and do serve in much broader capacities, including the highest position of all—Chief of Staff of the Air Force. Since the Air Force became a separate service in 1947, there have been twenty-one Chiefs of Staff—every single one of them has been a pilot.

This, too, needs to change if we are to win the war for innovation.

Having gathered all these facts and completed the initial Investigate phase on diversity and inclusion in the Air Force, the time came to Communicate and Activate.

My team was already putting together a variety of initiatives designed to encourage and increase diversity within the Air Force (and I picked up on a number of ideas myself while traveling and talking to women in the Air Force). At the same time, I thought it was important to let all airmen know what we, the senior leaders of the Air Force, intended to do and why it was important.

To this end, Chief of Staff General Mark Welsh, Chief Master Sergeant of the Air Force Jim Cody, and I sent two memos to all airmen in 2015. The first explained why we intended to focus more time on diversity and inclusion and how we—as a leadership team—were committed to this goal going forward. The second memo Activated nine initiatives to show we meant business. Within the next eighteen months, and with the help of Secretary of Defense Ash Carter, we Iterated by adding additional initiatives, plus we changed some important DOD policies.

Taken together, these changes were historic.
Here's some of what we did.

▶ An important policy change related to new mothers in the
Air Force. As I traveled, I repeatedly heard from women
that deployment and family issues were the top reasons
women left the Air Force at twice the rate of men at the
mid-career point. Specifically, we extended the time, from
six months to twelve months, that a new mother WOULD
NOT be subject to deployment or the retaking of the physical fitness test following the birth of a child. This was an
important accommodation for new mothers that would
help them balance the competing demands of family and
military service. I hope that it also eliminated the need for
women to take unhealthy actions so soon after childbirth
to return to the weight and physical fitness standards the
military requires;

▶ We launched the Career Intermission Program, which was
designed to retain high-quality airmen (both women and
men) by giving them the flexibility to transfer from active
duty to the reserve component for one to three years to
meet personal or professional needs. Afterwards, they
would return to active duty without losing their place in
line for promotion and would agree to serve for additional
years in return for participating in the program;

▶ By order of Secretary of Defense Ash Carter, all military
services doubled the amount of maternity leave for new
mothers from six to twelve paid weeks. (New fathers and
adopting parents were granted additional time off too,
though not as much as new birth mothers.) The maternity
leave position was a compromise between both Secretary

of the Navy, Ray Mabus, and me (we favored granting eighteen weeks) and the Army (especially the Chief of Staff), who wanted to limit the amount of time off for his soldiers because of readiness concerns. In any event, twelve weeks of paid maternity leave put the military in the top quartile of American employers when it came to time off for new mothers. Secretary Carter also directed all US-based Defense facilities with more than fifty employees to create designated lactation rooms for new mothers. (I couldn't help thinking back to those early days on the House Armed Services Committee when I pumped breast milk in the bathroom. Designated lactation rooms are a very welcome change!);

▶ Also, by order of the Secretary of Defense, all combat positions previously closed to women in the military were opened to all who could qualify for the high standards. Today, women have begun to compete for these newly opened positions, and a few have entered some of the career fields. I have no doubt that in the years to come, the ranks of women in these most difficult combat-oriented jobs will increase—and they will do a great job leading and executing;

▶ We made it easier for ROTC graduates of shorter stature (many of whom happened to be women) to apply to become pilots. I know this one sounds arcane, but remember I told you how underrepresented women are in the pilot career fields and how most of the top leaders in the Air Force are pilots?

▶ During the Investigate phase, we discovered that ROTC candidates did not have the same easy access as their Air Force

Academy counterparts to special measurement equipment that could facilitate the granting of a height waiver to fly in certain cockpits. Until, that is, we provided that measurement equipment during the ROTC summer camp. This one turned out to be an easy process fix;

▶ We changed the hiring process for our senior civilian personnel. Rather than allowing a single hiring manager to make the selection, we instituted civilian hiring panels consisting of at least three diverse individuals, not just with regard to race, gender, and ethnicity, but also with regard to background;

▶ We gave the Air Force Academy and the ROTC program directors a goal of building an officer applicant pool of 30 percent women (this was a five percentage point stretch compared to the applicant pool that existed at the time). Basically, this direction required Academy and ROTC leaders to do more early-outreach to ensure more qualified women applied to be officers in the Air Force. Over time, we reasoned, this would increase the percentage of women who would actually be selected to enter the Air Force as officers; and

▶ We launched the mentoring system "My Vector" within the Air Force and established two Secretary-led Lean In Circles. (I described both of these programs in some detail in Chapter 4.)

▶ Nearly from the start, we began the Iterate phase. In other words, as new ideas came to the forefront, we took action. By October 2016, the new Chief of Staff, General David Goldfein, Chief Master Sergeant Cody, and I launched the second set of diversity and inclusion initiatives that included:

- Mandatory gender bias training prior to key career events like promotion board meetings (for those who decide on promotions) and developmental team meetings (for those who decide on key assignments); and
- Adoption of the so-called "Rooney Rule" which required that a diverse slate of candidates be considered when making selections for key military developmental positions. (In 2003, Dan Rooney, the former Pittsburgh Steelers owner and chair of the NFL's diversity committee, was credited with instituting this requirement when interviewing for senior football operations jobs.)

As Follow Up, I conducted regular update meetings to receive progress reports on our Diversity initiatives. And we saw the beginning of change.

For example, during my tenure, we clearly increased the female officer applicant pool at the Academy and ROTC programs, though we fell slightly short of the 30 percent goal. Similarly, by the time I departed government service, there were 13,500 registered profiles and 6,000 mentoring connections established through MyVector.

But the key question is: how will this progress and these statistics actually relate to increasing diversity and inclusion within the Air Force ten years from now?

Many of these initiatives will take years to pay off (or not), and measuring progress will be difficult in some cases.

The bottom line is: It's impossible to judge at this time—but without consistent and long-term follow-up, these efforts and future approaches will surely fall by the wayside, and the Air Force will miss out on some terrific talent and innovation.

Before leaving the subject of diversity and inclusion, I want to tell you one more story—this one relates to a military personnel policy in flux.

When I became Secretary of the Air Force, the policy was that being a transgender individual was incompatible with military service. Transgender men and women could not join the military, and if they began identifying themselves as transgender once in the service, they could be involuntarily discharged (though there also was some flexibility to be retained). The reason was based on what turned out to be an outdated policy on mental health concerns. The "Don't Ask, Don't Tell" policy that limited gay and lesbian individuals from openly serving in the military had been changed years earlier, but the transgender prohibition lived on.

I remember vividly the first time I was asked about my views on this policy. I did an on-camera interview with Susan Page of *USA Today* who was asking me about a wide range of issues. The December 2014 interview probably lasted about forty-five minutes in all, though not that much survived for the broadcast piece. By way of background, I always prepared heavily for all press interviews and tried very hard to think through answers to what could be the most controversial questions.

But no preparation is perfect.

I didn't see this one coming, nor had I prepared. In the midst of questions about the campaign against ISIS in Iraq, the Air Force budget, and other themes for which I was totally prepared, Susan asked me my opinion about the ban on transgender individuals serving in the military.

Whether you are prepared for something or not, it's always important to remember your "authentic self." State what you truly believe. Even if the policy judgment is not your ultimate call to make, talk to your personal view, your belief system, your values.

I responded to Susan: "From my point of view, anyone who is capable of accomplishing the mission should be able to serve." Remembering that then-Secretary Chuck Hagel also seemed open to considering a change, I continued, "Times change. The policy is likely to come under review in the next year or so."

When the piece ran—in both print and broadcast via Capital Download—the headline and lead was "Air Force Secretary Supports Lifting Transgender Ban." Apparently, this was the first public statement of support from any Service Secretary about lifting the ban.

After this story broke, I was asked more frequently about the transgender service issue.

For example, I remember vividly being in Australia and conducting an All-Call with some of our Air Force personnel. One young man rose to ask a question about the transgender military service ban. He spoke about how some airmen are forced to hide their identities—was this fair and would it change?

I could tell that he was struggling personally—the audience reaction was a mix of snickers and eye rolling, but there was also head nodding and looks of sympathy from others.

I answered the question in much the same way as I had answered it before. I emphasized that the Air Force needed airmen that were smart, capable, hardworking, and dedicated to our core values. "If you have all that, then I want you in my Air Force," I said.

After the All-Call concluded, I took pictures and selfies with airmen (one of the really fun aspects about being Secretary of the Air Force). The same young airman approached me, stuffed a letter in my hand and asked me to read it when I had a moment. I then hopped in the car with the commanding officer of the base, and we drove off to our next stop.

While riding in the car, I read the letter. This airman declared to me that he was transgender. He loved his job, had excelled in his evaluations, and felt like a valued member of the team—by his boss and within his immediate unit. But he was leaving the Air Force because he could no longer remain within an organization whose stated policy was antithetical to who he was. He thanked me for my support for lifting the ban and asked me to keep pressing.

I turned to his Commanding officer and, without explaining why, I inquired about the airman who asked the transgender service question. The commander then told me the same basic story as the letter recounted—and that the commander had tried to talk the airman out of leaving precisely because he was such a valued contributor. But to no avail.

I can't say exactly how much time and money it took to recruit and train a replacement for this airman—but however much it was, it was too much. Which is why, during my tenure, I am proud the Department of Defense changed the policy going forward to allow transgender individuals to serve. I found that the best supporters of the new policy are those like the commanding officer in Australia—those that have direct knowledge of a transgender person. Those with no direct knowledge tend to fear the unknown.

The policy was changed following a lengthy review that included the leadership of the military services, medical and personnel experts, the Rand Corporation, and transgender personnel. Not only could qualified transgender individuals serve openly without fear of discharge, they could enter the military if they demonstrated two years of medical and psychological stability. The implementation of the policy was rolled out in stages over twelve months, including training for the rest of the force. The RAND Corporation did extensive work and demonstrated that the impact on military medical costs was diminutive and that readiness would not be impacted materially because of the small numbers involved (the RAND study estimated that between 1,320 and 6,630 transgender individuals were then serving in the active duty military, out of a total population of more than 1.3 million).

Then everything turned upside down.

The new transgender service policy, based on a methodical approach and extensive research, seemingly was tossed out the window with three successive tweets from President Trump in July 2017. He tweeted:

"After consultation with my Generals and military experts, please be advised that the United States Government will not accept or allow Transgender individuals to serve in any capacity in the US Military. Our military must be focused on decisive and overwhelming victory and cannot be burdened with the tremendous medical costs and disruption that transgender in the military would entail. Thank you."

It's still not clear what Generals President Trump consulted with. What is clear is that he did NOT consult with his Joint Chiefs of Staff. Fortunately, the Chairman of the Joint Chiefs, Marine General Joe Dunford, issued an internal memo to the nation's military leaders the very next day. (The other chiefs issued their own statements as well.)

The Dunford memo acknowledged that many must have questions about "yesterday's announcement." He went on to say that nothing would change based on a tweet. Rather the President needed to transmit direction to Secretary Mattis and that guidance would need to be translated into "implementation guidance." "In the meantime, we will continue to treat all our personnel with dignity and respect."

Translation: Steady as she goes, no changes based on tweets, keep doing your jobs, and don't let this distract you.

Secretary of Defense Jim Mattis (a four-star retired Marine General), also was reportedly not consulted and taken by surprise by the announcement. However, with that said, it now fell to him to back up these tweets with action.

So Secretary Mattis launched his own review and submitted a report to the White House.

Basically, the Mattis report—released by the White House in March 2018—contradicted all of our findings big time. For example, the new report cited "considerable scientific uncertainty" about gender dysphoria and went on to label transgender individuals "unfit" for military service. It also said that military cohesion, privacy, fairness, and safety would be sacrificed if transgender individuals were permitted to serve. Finally, the report said that the financial costs of permitting transgender individuals would burden the military healthcare system.

When questioned by the Congress, all military chiefs have contradicted the central tenet of the Mattis report—that the service of transgender individuals was harming military readiness.

The courts have stepped into this messy situation. At least four lawsuits are pending to block a reversal of the Obama-era transgender policy—former Navy Secretary Ray Mabus, Former Army Secretary Eric Fanning, and I are serving as expert witnesses in these cases. We were saddened by the policy reversal (and disagree strongly with the assertion that transgender individuals are a burden due to tremendous medical costs and a disruption to military readiness). We remain firmly committed to seeing the court cases through.

Treating all people with dignity and respect—regardless of race, gender, or sexual orientation—is the right thing to do and the smart thing to do when it comes to bolstering talent and innovation.

The final chapter on diversity and inclusion in the military has yet to be written.

## DIVERSITY PRODUCES REAL RESULTS

The business case for diversity from an organizational stand-point is robust, with many studies showing the benefits.

From a company financial performance perspective, research has shown:

- ▶ Globally, companies in the top quartile for gender diversity are 15 percent more likely to have financial returns above their respective national industry medians.

- ▶ Share prices of companies with at least one woman on the board outperformed those with no women.

- ▶ Fortune 500 companies with the most female directors outperformed those with the least number of female directors on return on invested capital by 26 percent.

- ▶ Having equal opportunities for professional growth in the workplace increases employee engagement, and companies with engaged employees grow revenue as much as 2.5 times more than those with low engagement.

Beyond financial success, additional research shows that diverse teams focus more on the facts and remain more objective, they process facts more carefully, and are more innovative. The benefits of diversity are numerous!

# CHAPTER 16

# Case Study 4: Supporting Pilots Who Don't Fly

Some of the Air Force's most important pilots never leave the face of the Earth. Remotely piloted aircraft pilots—known as drone pilots to most Americans but as RPA pilots in Air Force speak—were viewed by some as "stepchildren" within the Air Force. For years, this part of the force was not looked upon with equal prestige as those who flew "manned aircraft." Yet RPA pilots have been top contributors over the last decade in the war against terror.

Much of the intelligence, surveillance, reconnaissance (ISR), and precision strikes in places like Iraq, Afghanistan, Pakistan, and Syria (particularly against specific terrorists) have come from these unmanned systems. By the way, the term "unmanned" is a misnomer. Although there are no humans above the earth operating these aircraft, there are quite a few humans on the ground operating, surveilling, analyzing, and maintaining these systems.

RPA teams were, and still are, in extremely high demand by combat commanders around the world precisely because of the information and firepower they deliver. The demand was so high during my tenure, there came a time when we had to pull instructors from the schoolhouse in order to perform more missions. Because fewer instructors meant that fewer new drone pilots could be trained, we had entered a vicious cycle of fewer pilots working more missions. And many were beginning to vote with their feet as soon as they were able to choose whether or not to stay in the Air Force.

In June 2014, I traveled to Creech Air Force base in the vast Nevada desert and saw firsthand some of the RPA teams in action. This was an important piece of the Investigate part of the project.

Creech is a bare-bones Air Force base that lies about forty-five minutes to an hour drive from the larger Nellis Air Force Base and the city of Las Vegas. As a general proposition, most airmen prefer being stationed at Nellis—not at Creech.

Whereas Nellis has family housing and other amenities typical at stateside Air Force bases, Creech has none of this. In fact, no one actually lives at Creech, which means that everyone must commute on a daily basis back and forth from Nellis or from one of the communities near Nellis. This involves a long daily commute, though not longer (I originally reasoned) than what many face in major metropolitan areas with lots of traffic, like my home area of Washington, D.C. What was the big deal?

It turns out that the quality-of-life issues at Creech (and other remote RPA locations) coupled with the sheer pace of operations and the morale issues stemming from the perception of being second class pilots within the Air Force became a triple whammy that caused many to consider leaving the service. Add to this that opportunities in the civilian world were increasing, and you have a serious retention problem.

Let me give you a little more color on why the RPA force was so exhausted. RPA pilots were flying six days in a row, thirteen to fourteen hours per day, ranging from 900 to 1,100 flight-hours per year. Contrast that to the average pilot in one of the manned systems who, at the time, might have flown two hundred to three hundred hours per year.

Moreover, RPA pilots were engaged in particularly stressful missions, the most stressful of which typically happened in the middle of the night. To fully understand this, you need to remember that they are sitting in darkened trailers, watching people and places halfway around the world, mostly when it is daylight in the Middle East and Africa. The aircraft remain aloft for long periods of time, so the pilots and analysts can track and understand patterns of life on the ground. Who are the bad guys and what are their habits? When do innocent civilians wander into the scene? It's extremely important to distinguish between the two because the US military will only strike when there is a high level of confidence that it is striking the RIGHT target—and that the potential for causing innocent loss of life is MINIMAL. Even after a weapon is launched against a terror target, if an innocent suddenly walks onto the scene, the strike can be aborted by diverting the weapon.

So the stakes are high, mistakes can be very costly, and all of this weighs heavily on RPA pilots. Finally, at the conclusion of a stressful duty day, they begin the long drive home, get a few hours of sleep, and then try to interact with their families as though they had not been in a war zone a few hours earlier.

Psychologically, that's a hard thing to do—harder than actually being deployed to a war zone and separated from family for a matter of months. When you are separated, you can totally focus on the mission for the period of deployment. When you return home daily, you need to switch back and forth between "hunter/killer" and "Mom/Dad" in just a few hours.

Upon returning from Creech, we started building a set of actions designed to address the immediate shortfalls within the RPA community. We also had our eye on some longer-term solutions but knew that these would have to wait. General Hawk Carlisle, Commander of the Air Combat Command with responsibility for the RPA community, was key to this overall effort and was the first senior leader to voice serious concern about the health of the community. Lisa Disbrow, the new Undersecretary of the Air Force who took over after Eric Fanning moved to a new assignment, was absolutely critical in managing some of the thorniest issues affecting the RPA community within the halls of the Pentagon.

By January 2015, we were ready to Communicate and Activate. After giving a heads-up to the Congressional committees with the greatest interest in the RPA world, Air Force Chief of Staff, General Welsh, and I held a "State of the Air Force" press conference. We outlined the challenge and the immediate problem at hand—then we laid out specific steps to begin to remedy the RPA pilot shortage, including increasing RPA pilot numbers by utilizing more part time National Guard forces and contractor personnel. To help retention, we also announced modest pay increases, recognizing that pay was an issue, though not the top issue. We promised that more would follow in the next few months.

And we kept that promise. This is where Iterate began to kick in.

General Carlisle launched the Culture and Process Improvement Program—CPIP for short—which was modeled after the focus group approach we took with the nuclear enterprise. And just as we found in the nuclear enterprise, there were important quality-of-life issues that we needed to address, not only for pilots but also for others who support this mission.

For example, the relatively few locations where RPA airmen could be based meant that airmen and families felt "stuck" without the opportunity to rotate to new places. (This reminded me on some level of what the nuclear airmen were saying.) Because the force was constantly under pressure to perform the mission, there was precious little time for professional development opportunities. Finally, the schoolhouse issue came up repeatedly. How could the number of RPA pilots grow if instructors are performing the mission and not instructing new trainees?

Ultimately, we announced more "get well" fixes for the RPA force:

▶ We secured a temporary decrease to the RPA workload—called combat air patrols. This action gave the force a breather and allowed instructors to return to the schoolhouse and produce more new RPA pilots;

▶ Now that the number of new pilots was on the rise, we announced the formation of new units and basing locations for the future. Over time, 2,500 to 3,500 new airmen will be added to the force;

▶ We added professional development opportunities for RPA personnel;

▶ We announced a new $35,000 annual retention bonus; and

▶ We opened one category of remotely piloted aircraft to *enlisted pilots*.

Without question, this last initiative was the most controversial of all because it represented a major culture shift for the Air Force. You see, ever since the Air Force became a separate military service in 1947, the pilot career field has always been for officers and officers alone.

That was about to change and step one was to introduce enlisted pilots into the world of the Global Hawk.

By way of background, during my time as Secretary, there were three types of RPAs in the Air Force inventory:

- ▶ MQ-1 Predator: this aircraft was reaching the end of its life (it was subsequently phased out in March 2018). The Predator began as a surveillance aircraft, but later models were modified over time to carry weapons.

- ▶ MQ-9 Reaper: this drone will be in the inventory until the 2030s. It goes farther and faster than the Predator and provides both enhanced surveillance and increased strike capability over the Predator.

- ▶ RQ4 Global Hawk: this aircraft flies higher than both the Predator and Reaper. Therefore, it can surveil a wider swath of the earth. The Global Hawk has no strike capability.

We selected the Global Hawk to be the first test case for the introduction of enlisted pilots because it had a more stable training program at the time than the other two types. In addition, as Global Hawk does not have strike capability, we avoided the debate about giving enlisted personnel decision authority over conducting a strike. In today's Air Force, that decision rests solely with officers, and it goes against the grain of many (though not me) that this authority might be yielded to enlisted members.

After I made the initial decision, General Carlisle and his team took about six months to develop a specific implementation plan, including how we would select Global Hawk pilots from the enlisted force, how they would be trained and how we would develop their careers. The initiative began small, literally with four pilots trained in the first wave, but will grow beyond this as lessons are learned and the Air Force becomes increasingly comfortable with the idea.

Which, once again, is why <u>Follow Up</u> and measurement on all these areas is so vital.

Toward the end of my tenure, I made a return trip to Creech to see how some of the changes were playing within the community. I would characterize the mood as one of cautious optimism. The team was aware of all the changes coming down the pike (thanks to the <u>Communicate</u> part) but had not felt the direct impact of all the changes yet.

I also had the opportunity to visit with the first four enlisted Global Hawk pilot candidates at Initial Flight Training School in Pueblo, Colorado. They were at the very beginning part of their training, but so far, so good.

Flash forward to today: The health of the RPA force is much better. The schoolhouse is manned at 100 percent, and the take-rates on the higher retention bonuses have improved. This means the Air Force is producing and retaining enough new RPA pilots that there is no longer a need to draw from the pool of new manned pilots to meet the mission. Overall, the manpower numbers are up in this community, which means that all should have somewhat of a less demanding schedule.

Locations in Florida and South Carolina have been selected to host new RPA units, which will afford airmen who support this mission with more basing options in the future. And there are now eleven enlisted airmen flying RPA missions, with a projection of a hundred by 2020—representing roughly half the Global Hawk force.

## ENGAGEMENT MAKES A BIG DIFFERENCE IN EVERY ORGANIZATION

If the RPA community had been part of the private sector, some might have said they were not sufficiently "engaged." There is more to engagement than being extremely busy.

Bain & Company has identified that employee engagement is a combination of employee satisfaction and employee inspiration. Satisfied and inspired employees are "long-term value creators" in an organization, making improving employee engagement a worthwhile investment.

Employee satisfaction involves ensuring that employees feel valued and supported and that they have what they need to be successful. Inspired employees bring energy, enthusiasm, and creativity to work and fuel productivity and innovation. Engaged employees, those who are both satisfied and inspired, stay longer, recruit friends, and help build the organization's brand.

Focusing on these components of engagement has been shown to decrease attrition, improve organizations' ability to achieve their goals and serve their stakeholders, and foster environments of feedback across the organization.

# CHAPTER 17

# Case Study 5: Stop Doing Stuff

I HAVE LEARNED MULTIPLE TIMES throughout my life that, in my zeal to get things done, it is equally important to stop doing stuff. If you try to do everything by yourself to the same level of excellence, you will soon experience overload and perform in a suboptimal way across the board. In Chapter 7, I explained that as a parent, I established priorities and literally outsourced the stuff that I decided to stop doing (e.g. laundry, food shopping, and cleaning). This freed up my most precious resource—my time—so that I could devote more of it to my children while I was at home.

The same point holds true in business and government.

When we were working on the details of the SAIC spin, we became sensitized to the need to stop doing stuff. At that time, SAIC had hundreds of written processes, procedures, and training requirements. We called them "SAIC Instructions." Some of these were generated from law or government regulation and others were generated by the functional staffs of the company.

Process, procedure, and training can be fantastic—clearly, all organizations need some of this—and government contractors need more than most in order to comply with the complex legal and regulatory environment in Washington, D.C.

But if all of this becomes a massive time suck, saps too much energy from the team, and provides questionable value-add to the organization, management needs to sit up and take notice.

SAIC, like many other corporations, had gradually moved away from being what I call a "high-touch environment" (in which many employees received human help with everything from admin support to HR assistance), to more of a "self-serve environment" in which employees were expected to do more of these jobs by themselves. While this approach certainly can be cost effective (because overhead resources can be reduced), it can hurt productivity and morale if employees get too bogged down in activities they were not hired to do.

During the spin, we found that one of the keys was to stop doing stuff—which, believe me, is easier said than done. We ended up going back to basics on all process, procedure, and training requirements. We asked ourselves: Who said we have to do this? If the answer was the law, or a government requirement, we kept the instruction. If the answer was, "SAIC said so," or worse yet, "That's the way we've always done it," we put that instruction under a microscope to ensure that we really needed to keep it going forward.

This effort was painful—there wasn't a single process or training requirement that didn't add some value, and each inevitably had a proponent within the company who would argue to keep it in place at all costs. But in the end, we were able to streamline and consolidate SAIC instructions based on this process.

We also recognized that the company would be challenged in the years to come to ensure that more stuff didn't creep back into the mix without top leaders knowing about it. So we set up a decision matrix that would need to be followed in the event any functional staff wished to add a new training or process requirement down the line.

And, of course, we told SAICers what we were doing so that they would know that management listened to their input and was taking action.

I faced a similar problem as Secretary of the Air Force.

Almost from the beginning of my tenure, I heard about additional duties and other non-mission requirements that took up a lot of airmen's time.

I first heard the word "queep" at an All-Call during the question and answer period. The question came from a member of the part-time National Guard.

"Ma'am, you say your top priorities are taking care of people and making the Air Force more efficient. My question is: what are you doing to attack queep?"

I had no idea what he was talking about, so I had to ask, "What is queep?"

"Ma'am, it's all the extra stuff we have to do, like paperwork and computer-based training—that sort of thing. I'm a maintainer, so I'm supposed to spend my time working on aircraft. But I can't get at it this drill weekend because I have to complete my training on the new travel reimbursement system. And it works like crap, by the way."

Everyone laughed, including me, because it was unusual for anyone to say crap in front of the Secretary of the Air Force.

"I'm afraid I don't know anything about this," I admitted, "but let me get back to you on it."

This was not unusual for me—there were lots of topics I didn't know about at this stage. So rather than try to give a non-answer, my military assistant would take a note, research the matter and get back to the commander at a later time so that he or she could share the answer with others. Eventually, we provided a response about the Defense Travel System (DTS), a new self-service IT system that allowed military personnel to create travel orders, prepare reservations, receive approvals, and get reimbursements. True, it had been newly introduced to National Guard units, which were not really used to it yet, and there were some bugs in the system that needed to be ironed out.

Training on DTS, however, turned out to be just the tip of the iceberg of a bigger problem.

And I completely failed to see that bigger problem at first.

The issue of too much non-mission stuff kept coming up again and again. In addition to "queep," I heard airmen complain about "additional duties," computer-based training requirements, and other processes and procedures which they clearly believed made no sense. And when combined, all of these requirements were sapping time, energy, and morale from the team.

I finally raised the issue with the Chief of Staff, General Welsh. He was well aware of the issue and was committed to tackling it head on.

But here's where we made a big mistake.

Unlike at SAIC, where we first gathered all instructions and then parsed those we imposed on ourselves versus those we followed for legal or regulatory compliance reasons—we launched the Air Force effort on the basis of anecdotal information from airmen alone. And then we tasked the Air Staff, the equivalent of the corporate staff in the private sector, with reviewing additional duties, process, and procedure to determine what we could stop doing.

In retrospect, the Investigate part of our approach was not adequate, and we gave the task of solving the problem to the very people who were most likely to favor keeping most of the status quo. This eventually became clear to me, but not in the beginning. So, unfortunately, we had a false start and ended up wasting time.

After tasking the Air Staff, I began to <u>Communicate</u> in All-Calls that we were on the case. General Welsh and other senior leaders did the same. As time went by, we became anxious to <u>Activate</u> and kept asking for progress updates. It was taking way too long, which, in hindsight, was a major red flag.

Probably six months later, the Air Staff presented us with a decision brief to stop doing stuff. To say that I was very disappointed in the product would be an understatement. They presented their methodology and concluded that just about everything was either required by law or regulation and that the few areas over which the Air Force could exert control were so essential that we had to keep almost all of them. In fairness, there were a handful of things we could stop doing, but I remember feeling that these few things would not have much of an impact on the overall problem, so I opted not to make a public announcement on the matter.

I gave some thought to bringing in an outside firm to help us with a follow-on effort (realizing now that the Air Staff had been the wrong people to take the lead on the project), but we were pinching every penny in those days, so I let the idea drop. Mentally, I placed it in the "too hard" category and moved on to other matters.

I had given up too quickly, but luckily, General Welsh came back later with a much better approach. You might call this the <u>Iterate</u> part of the effort.

As Chief, he met with wing commanders periodically throughout the year. For context, if the US Air Force were a corporation, wings and their subordinate units (squadrons) would be the business units of the company. General Welsh challenged his team of wing commanders to give him an actionable list of things they felt we could stop doing—and they did just that.

We took the list generated by the wing commanders and separated the items into two groups: 1) those required by either law or Department of Defense policy; and 2) those we imposed upon ourselves. And then we focused as first order of business on the items over which we had total control.

I learned for the first time that there was an actual Air Force Instruction (AFI 38-206) that imposed a whopping sixty-one additional duties on airmen in every unit, even though these duties typically did not relate to the core mission of the unit.

For example, there was a requirement that every unit designate and train a "Treaty Compliance Officer" even though most units across the Air Force had no work related to compliance with treaties.

Similarly, every unit was required to designate and train an airman to be the "Contamination Control Team Member." To be sure, this was a very important job if the team had responsibilities for nuclear, chemical, or biological decontamination operations, but not very useful for those units that did not.

"Awards/Recognition Program Manager" was another time-consuming additional duty—per AFI 38-206, every unit in the Air Force was required to have one of these as well.

Remember the Defense Travel System issue? In addition to every airman learning and performing functions on the system, each unit was required to designate and train one or more "Lead Organizational Defense Travel System Administrators" to review and approve travel vouchers and orders within their units.

Finally—my personal favorite—every unit was required to designate and train a "Unit Tax Representative" to help others in preparing and filing their income taxes! You can probably imagine, during tax season, this became a near-full-time job—and I remind you that all of these examples were additional duties on top of the airman's other full-time job.

By the time we were finally ready to Activate our plan to reduce additional duties, General Welsh had retired but the new Chief, General David Goldfein, was fully on board. In August 2016, General Goldfein and I issued a Memorandum to all Airmen in which we announced the elimination, reduction, or reassignment of twenty-nine of the sixty-one additional duties.

We made clear that this was Part I of our effort to return precious time to our people. Part II and beyond would come from the new "Airmen's Time" task force we created that would review computer-based training and other requirements that detract from the mission as well as ensure that new requirements didn't creep back in.

We announced the return of commander support staffs (CSS) to assist with administrative duties (much like in corporate America, these staffs had been cut way back over the years).

Finally, most important of all, in recognition that CSS teams would take time to build back up, we empowered Commanders "to discontinue any non-critical duties beyond their ability to resource."

Stated another way: if it's not value-added to your mission, stop doing it!

With this directive, the "Treaty Compliance Officer" and "Contamination Control Team Member" requirements were eliminated as across the board mandates and instead required only in those units that dealt with the issues at hand. Much is now left to the judgment of the individual commanders.

The "Awards/Recognition Program Manager" requirement was reassigned to the commander support staff.

The "Unit Tax Representative" was eliminated outright.

And while airmen still needed to manage their own travel on DTS, the functionality had improved, and the requirement for "Lead Organizational Travel System Administrator" was shifted to the commander support staff.

We <u>Communicated</u> the message of commander empowerment and elimination of additional duties at every juncture. As it turned out, implementation was slower than I expected because many commanders did not know what to make of it. Risk aversion was so strong, they weren't sure they believed it.

What if I eliminate this duty and then get slammed by the Inspector General (the equivalent of internal audit in the private sector)? What if I encounter some other blowback for eliminating this function? What if this? What if that?

For some, continuing on the same path was easier and safer than seizing upon the new empowerment.

Sometimes, airmen would tell me at All-Calls that duties had not been eliminated per the directive. I would then follow up with their commander who would tell me that his hands were tied. After a while, I began carrying around my own memo with the relevant sentence underlined in yellow to prove that commanders did have the authority to stop doing stuff.

"So exercise it!" I told them.

The "Airmen's Time" task force was critical for the <u>Iterate</u> part of the job. I asked my Assistant Secretary for Manpower, Gabe Camarillo, to oversee this effort to ensure we produced more change before our time in government was up.

The task force took on the challenge of reviewing computer-based and "ancillary" training, another source of great dissatisfaction within the force. As part of their <u>Investigate</u> phase, the task force identified forty-two required training courses (representing sixty hours of time if all were taken in a single year) and put out a survey to the field to get a sense of which were viewed as most burdensome and least value added. It became crystal clear that a lot of required training was duplicative of training or knowledge airmen could or should acquire elsewhere.

Armed with this information, we were ready to launch Part II of the initiative to Stop Doing Stuff. In October 2016, General Goldfein and I put out guidance eliminating fifteen standalone training courses (including nine of the ten identified by airman as most burdensome) and consolidating or streamlining sixteen others. Of the sixteen, two will have "test out" options for those who have taken the courses before and know the material, four will be conducted less frequently, one will be consolidated with another, and nine will be shortened.

Among the training eliminated as duplicative or unnecessary:

1. Air Force Inspection System—an introduction to the role of the Inspector General;
2. Base Emergency Preparedness Orientation;
3. Fire Extinguisher Safety Training; and
4. Safety course—Initial training for Motorcycle operators.

Training courses streamlined or reduced included:

1. Chemical, biological, radiological, and nuclear awareness training;
2. Religious Freedom computer training;
3. Self-Aid and Buddy Care;
4. Safety Course—Driver improvement and Rehabilitation; and
5. My personal favorites: three separate courses about the Defense Travel System!

All of this was a good start, but the work must continue and Follow Up is crucial. And it is. Most recently, in May 2018, the new Air Force leadership put out a third piece of guidance that continues the theme of giving time back to airmen.

"Effective immediately, commanders and supervisors are empowered to conduct nearly all mandatory ancillary training as they see fit," directed my successor, Secretary of the Air Force, Heather Wilson, Chief Goldfein, and Chief Master Sergeant Kaleth Wright. In theory, this guidance should allow for more streamlining and flexibility to offer briefings in lieu of computer-based training or vice versa.

The war against queep continues!

## ANOTHER FORM OF QUEEP

Organizational drag, or "queep" is a significant issue in the private sector too.

In addition to non-value-added paperwork and training requirements, Bain & Company found that the average company loses 20 percent of its productive capacity, one business day a week, due to unnecessary or inefficient collaboration.

What is driving this drag?

**Lack of scheduling control**—the average manager has less than seven hours of uninterrupted productive time each week. Time consumed by meetings and email is growing by ~8 percent annually, crowding out deep-thinking time, and more than 40 percent of this time is unnecessary and could be reduced or eliminated.

**Productivity declines with scale**—for every 10 percent increase in employee population, productivity decreases by 2 percent.

Bain identified five best practices for managing organizational time:

1. Simplify the organization to eliminate unnecessary interactions.
2. Align the organization to make necessary interactions more efficient and effective.
3. Create a time budget from scratch, with clear delegation of authority for all time investments.
4. Require business cases for all new projects and explicit criteria for ending initiatives.
5. Provide real-time feedback data to manage organizational load.

# The BLUF (Revisited)

IN *AIM HIGH*, I OFFERED YOU MY FRAMEWORK for achieving professional and personal success and fulfillment. Although I gave you the Bottom Line Up Front (BLUF) in Chapter 1, there were many stories throughout the book containing additional insights and tips.

So the final chapter is the BLUF Revisited.

Remember, there are three essential actions, with strategies to pursue within each.

Just to recap, here they are once more, this time with the insights and tips captured for easy reference.

### Chart and Navigate Your Path

1. **Make a Plan A, But Prepare to Zig-Zag**
   - Create a roadmap of where you want to go in life—this is your Plan A—then work toward it.
   - Have big aspirations—something we women don't always do.

- If Plan A fails (or turns out to not be right for you), Zig-Zag to Plan B.
- Be open to new possibilities and take risks. When one door closes, another opens. You must walk through that door.
- Resilience—bouncing back no matter what, is a key skill.

2. **Be part of Something Big**
   - Having a purpose is key to feeling fulfilled in life.
   - Purpose can be anything that jazzes you.
   - Money is important, but it will not give you purpose.
   - Look for ways to contribute to the well-being or betterment of others.
   - Invest in your personal and professional relationships—they are critical for your success and happiness.

3. **Get A Mentor; Be A Mentor; Build Your Network**
   - Mentors and your network can contribute big time to your success
   - A mentor can be anyone who does something you aspire to do—go on the offense and get one!
   - Ask someone to join you for coffee—listen to their story.
   - Pay mentorship forward: Be a mentor—even start a program—as soon as you are able.

4. **Hang in There with Positivity**
   - No one likes a Debbie Downer.
   - Embrace change, at least for a while. Adapt to new approaches and management styles.

- Leave a position only if you can't make the new assignment (or boss's style) work for you.
- Learn positive lessons from negative experiences.
- Take care with your words and body language.
- Understand the factors that drive difficult personalities. This will help you empathize and not take bad behavior personally.
- Perform solid due diligence on the new boss before accepting an assignment.

5. **Learn, Evolve, Reinvent**
   - Keep learning throughout your career: take short courses; apply for company training programs; volunteer for new or rotational assignments; do your research.
   - Leverage the knowledge of your mentors and network as part of your lifelong learning.
   - Practice your elevator pitch—that is, explain the value you bring to your organization—and keep evolving it as you grow.

6. **Lead A Full Life Beyond Work**
   - Having a purpose-driven private life is essential.
   - When managing the work/life balance, make priorities and stick with them.
   - Don't try to do everything by yourself.
   - Accept that good enough is good enough when it comes to household chores.
   - The gift of time is the best gift of all.
   - Invest in experiences more than things.

- Let go of guilt.
- Depending on where you are in life, try "special time," take "kidnap weekends," and block more "me time."

## Lead and Inspire Teams

1. **Speak Up And Listen Deeply**
   - Public speaking skills become more important as you advance in your career. Polish these skills.
   - Here are some public speaking tips:
     o Keep it simple (Three or four main points).
     o Tell stories.
     o Authenticity and passion go a long way.
     o Self-deprecating humor usually works best.
     o Practice your delivery and don't be afraid to repeat.
   - Leading teams requires deep listening and accepting input.
   - Get to know your team as real people—this will show that you care and help you empathize.
   - Learn to read non-verbal signals.
   - Effective communication can help women overcome the "likeability penalty"

2. **Role Model Ethical Behavior**
   - Ethics is both an individual and a team sport.
   - Just because you hold a senior position doesn't mean you should feel entitled.
   - Don't put up with jerks.
   - Proactive communication is essential when dealing with an ethical crisis.
   - Don't compromise on ethics. Period.

3. **Put People First**
   - If you get the people part of the equation right, the rest (like strategy and technology) is more likely to fall into place.
   - As a leader, you must help your entire team navigate the change journey.
   - Your team must be engaged and felt heard throughout the process.
   - Use focus groups to engage.
   - Take care to ensure that top performers don't get lost within the policies and processes of a large organization.

4. **Play to Your Strengths Within a Great Team**
   - Know what your key strengths and talents are—and what they are not.
   - Play to your strengths, but always within a great team.
   - Hallmarks of a great team are:
     - Members have diverse backgrounds and experience. Each needs to give and get.
     - The team has a clear vision and shared goals.
     - Individuals have energy and drive, especially in difficult circumstances.
     - Celebrate successes, learn from failures; the leader accepts responsibility on behalf of the team.
     - Members have passion for their work and for each other.

## Get Things Done

1. **Investigate**
   - Gather facts and input from multiple perspectives.
   - Understand the urgency and complexity of the challenge.
   - Consider the use of focus groups to gather opinions.
   - Get used to ambiguity (you will never have all the facts).
   - Review courses of action.

2. **Communicate**
   - Build the case for action; obtain buy in from your team.
   - Make the case—and don't rely on the written word alone.
   - Invest substantial personal time.
   - Keep repeating the top messages.

3. **Activate**
   - Start small and scale.
   - Focus on what you can control.
   - Double down on people issues.

4. **Iterate**
   - When making a change or starting something new, recognize that you won't get it completely right on the first pass.
   - Prepare to add, subtract, or otherwise alter your first plan depending on what works and does not work.

5. Follow Up
   - Once and done is never the answer.
   - Remain firm in your direction—be relentless. Change takes years.
   - Invest personal time in reviewing progress—and let everyone know you are doing so.
   - Measure everything possible.

SUBMITTED MY RESIGNATION as the twenty-third Secretary of the Air Force on January 20, 2017—at the conclusion of the Obama Administration.

But even now, I return to the Pentagon from time to time, especially for promotion or retirement ceremonies for the people who were special to me.

Today, as I walk through the fourth-floor SECAF corridor—"within the glass doors," as airmen say—a new portrait hangs on the wall—it's mine—along with the twenty-one men and one woman who preceded me in this important and unforgettable role.

And I owe it all to my formula.

As I have said before, these actions and strategies have worked for me—personally and professionally—to survive and thrive through change and dysfunction. I hope they will help you too.

Now let's get busy.

*Aim High!*

# Acknowledgments

Writing *Aim High* has been a journey—and I'm grateful that I did not travel alone. Fortunately, I got the people part of this equation right!

My family (Frank, Sam, Regina, and Regina Gail) gave me love and support throughout the arduous book writing process and each provided important editorial comments along the way. I love you guys and I will be forever grateful!

Manny Maceda, the Worldwide Managing Partner of Bain & Company, made it possible for Jen Hayes, Melissa Artabane, and Shalini Chudasama to support me in this effort. These women provided the data that support the stories and lessons learned throughout the book and are the authors of the "data boxes." Jen, Melissa, and Shalini also gave me invaluable editorial comment along the way. Thank you, Bain!

All former senior government officials must submit book manuscripts through their former agencies for a security review. I was fortunate that Carolyn Oredugba and Pat Zarodkiewicz—two fantastic Air Force civilians—handled my review in an expeditious and professional manner.

Major Becky Heyse, who supported me in Public Affairs when I was Secretary of the Air Force, was instrumental in helping assemble many of the photographs that appear in *Aim High*. I could not have pulled all of this together without Becky's assistance.

Sheryl Sandberg is a role model for so many—including me—and I am grateful not only for her friendship, but also for the Lean In movement she founded.

My agent, Ken Lizotte, and editor, Debra Englander, were critical in helping me tell this story and find my voice as an author.

Finally, I have one exciting update to share. Regina gave birth in February 2019 to a baby girl, Liana Blair. I finally have a little one to call me Grandma and who will, one day, *Aim High* on her own!

# Works Cited

## Chapter 2: Make a Plan A, But Prepare to Zig-Zag

Artabane, Melissa, Julie Coffman, and Darci Darnell. 2017. "Charting the Course: Getting Women to the Top." Bain & Company, January 31, 2017. https://www.bain.com/insights/charting-the-course -women-on-the-top/.

Garton, Eric, and Michael Mankins. 2017. *Time, Talent, Energy: Overcome Organizational Drag and Unleash your Team's Productive Power.* Boston: Harvard Business School Publishing.

Sandberg, Sheryl, and Adam Grant. 2017. *OPTION B: Facing Adversity, Building Resilience, and Finding Joy.* New York: Alfred A Knopf.

## Chapter 3: Be Part of Something Big

Artabane, Melissa, Julie Coffman, and Darci Darnell. 2017. "Charting the Course: Getting Women to the Top." Bain & Company, January 31, 2017. https://www.bain.com/insights/charting-the-course -women-on-the-top/.

Schawbel, Dan. 2015. "The Millennial Leadership Survey." *WorkplaceTrends,* July 20, 2015. https://workplacetrends.com/the-millennial -leadership-survey.

## Chapter 4: Get a Mentor, Be a Mentor, Build your Network

Foust-Cummings, Heather, Sarah Dinolfo, and Jennifer Kohler. 2011. *Sponsoring Women to Success.* New York: Catalyst.

Hewlett, Sylvia Ann. 2011. *The Real Benefit of Finding a Sponsor.* Boston: Harvard Business Review.

Sonnenberg, Lauren. 2018. "How to Turn a Mentor Into a Sponsor." *Forbes,* June 8, 2018. https://www.forbes.com/sites/laurensonnenberg /2018/06/08/how-to-turn-a-mentor-into-a-sponsor/#1ef59c066e2f.

## Chapter 5: Hang In There with Positivity

Artabane, Melissa, Julie Coffman, and Darci Darnell. 2017. "Charting the Course: Getting Women to the Top." Bain & Company, January 31, 2017. https://www.bain.com/insights/charting-the-course -women-on-the-top/.

Garton, Eric. 2017. "How to Be an Inspiring Leader." *Harvard Business Review,* April 25, 2017. https://hbr.org/2017/04/how-to-be-an-inspiring -leader.

## Chapter 6: Learn, Evolve, Reinvent

Carpenter, Julia. 2018. "The Power of More than One Woman on a Board." *CNN Money,* July 25, 2018. https://money.cnn.com/2018/07/02/pf/ women-boards-representation/index.html.

Kramer, Vicki W., Alison M. Konrad, and Sumru Erkut. 2006. *Critical Mass on Corporate Boards: Why Three or More Women Enhance Governance.* Boston: Wellesley Centers For Women.

Lee, Linda-Eling, Ric Marshall, Damion Rallis, and Matt Moscardi. 2015. "Women on Boards." MSCI, November 2015. https://www.msci.com/ documents/10199/04b6f646-d638-4878-9c61-4eb91748a82b.

Rigby, Darrell K, Jeff Sutherland, and Hirotaka Takeuchi. 2016. "Embracing Agile." *Harvard Business Review,* May 2016. 40-48, 50.

## Chapter 7: Lead a Full Life Beyond Work

Artabane, Melissa, Julie Coffman, and Darci Darnell. 2017. "Charting the Course: Getting Women to the Top." Bain & Company, January 31, 2017. https://www.bain.com/insights/charting-the-course -women-on-the-top/.

Fajardo, Catalina, and Maureen Erasmus. 2017. "Gender (Dis)parity in South Africa." Bain & Company, May 24, 2017. https://www.bain. com/insights/gender-disparity-in-south-africa/.

Sandberg, Sheryl. 2013. *Lean In: Women, Work, and the Will to Lead.* New York: Alfred A Knopf.

## Chapter 8: Speak Up and Listen Deeply

Eagly, Alice H. 2013. "Women as Leaders: Leadership Style Versus Leaders' Values and Attitudes." *Gender & Work: Challenging Conventional Wisdom.* Boston: Harvard Business School.

Gastil, John. 1994. "A Definition and Illustration of Democratic Leadership." *Human Relations* 47 (8): 953-975.

Korn Ferry Hay Group. 2016. *Women Outperform Men in 11 of 12 Key Emotional Intelligence Competencies.* Los Angeles: Korn Ferry.

Miller, Claire Cain. 2016. "Women Actually Do Govern Differently." *The New York Times,* November 10, 2016. https://www.nytimes.com/2016/11/10/upshot/women-actually-do-govern-differently.html.

Rhee, Kenneth S., and Tracey H. Sigler. 2015. "Untangling the Relationship Between Gender and Leadership." *Gender in Management: An International Journal* 30 (2): 109-134.

## Chapter 9: Role Model Ethical Behavior

Aveta Business Institute. n.d. "The Importance and Advantages of Good Business Ethics." Accessed July 2018. https://www.sixsigmaonline.org/six-sigma-training-certification-information/the-importance-and-advantages-of-good-business-ethics.

Kray, Laura J., and Michael P. Haselhuhn. 2012. "Male Pragmatism in Negotiators' Ethical Reasoning." *Journal of Experimental Social Psychology* 48: 1124-1131.

## Chapter 10: Put People First

Garton, Eric. 2017. "How to Be an Inspiring Leader." *Harvard Business Review,* April 25, 2017. https://hbr.org/2017/04/how-to-be-an-inspiring-leader.

## Chapter 11: Play to Your Strengths Within a Great Team

Garton, Eric, and Michael Mankins. 2017. *Time, Talent, Energy: Overcome Organizational Drag and Unleash Your Team's Productive Power.* Boston: Harvard Business School Publishing.

## Chapter 13: Case Study 1: The Nuclear Enterprise

Delizonna, Laura. 2017. "High-Performing Teams Need Psychological Safety. Here's How to Create It." *Harvard Business Review,* August 24, 2017. https://hbr.org/2017/08/high-performing-teams-need-psychological-safety-heres-how-to-create-it.
Rozovsky, Julia. 2015. "The Five Keys to a Successful Google Team." Google re:Work, November 17, 2015. https://rework.withgoogle.com/blog/five-keys-to-a-successful-google-team.

## Chapter 14: Case Study 2: Fighting Sexual Assault and Harassment

Joyful Heart Foundation. n.d. "6 Steps to Support a Survivor." Accessed July 2018. http://www.joyfulheartfoundation.org/6-steps-to-support-a-survivor.
Kearl, Holly. 2018. *The Facts Behind the #MeToo Movement: A National Study on Sexual Harassment and Assault.* Reston: Stop Street Harassment.
Option B. n.d. "Three ways to get involved." Accessed July 2018. https://optionb.org/about.
Option B. n.d. "How to Support a Friend After Sexual Assault." Accessed July 2018. https://optionb.org/build-resilience/advice/how-to-support-a-friend-after-sexual-assault.

## Chapter 15: Case Study 3: Making the Air Force More Diverse

Carter, Nancy M., and Harvey M. Wagner. 2011. *The Bottom Line: Corporate Performance and Women's Representation on Boards (2004–2008).* New York: Catalyst.

Credit Suisse. 2012. "Large-Cap Companies with at Least One Woman on the Board Have Outperformed Their Peer Group with No Women on the Board by 26% over the Last Six Years, According to a Report by Credit Suisse Research Institute." Media Relations Credit Suisse AG, news release, July 31, 2012. https://www.credit-suisse.com/corporate/en/articles/media-releases/42035-201207.html.

Hunt, Vivian, Dennis Layton, and Sara Prince. 2015. *Why Diversity Matters*. McKinsey & Company.

Korn Ferry Institute. 2016. "Measures for Success." Reports & Insights, April 18, 2016. https://www.kornferry.com/institute/measures-for-success.

Rock, David, and Heidi Grant. 2016. "Why Diverse Teams Are Smarter." *Harvard Business Review*, November 4, 2016. https://hbr.org/2016/11/why-diverse-teams-are-smarter.

## Chapter 16: Case Study 4: Supporting Pilots Who Don't Fly

Bain & Company. n.d. "The Employee Net Promoter System." Accessed July 2018. http://www.netpromotersystem.com/about/employee-engagement.aspx.

## Chapter 17: Case Study 5: Stop Doing Stuff

Garton, Eric, and Michael Mankins. 2017. *Time, Talent, Energy: Overcome Organizational Drag and Unleash your Team's Productive Power*. Boston: Harvard Business School Publishing.